The Wow! Mathematics

SATs Revision

Paul Broadbent

Good day. I'm Sir Ralph Witherbottom. I'm an accomplished inventor, a dashing discoverer and an enthusiastic entrepreneur.

Hi! I'm Isabella Witherbottom – my friends call me Izzy. I'm Sir Ralph's daughter and I like to keep him on his toes!

And they both keep me on my toes! How do you do? I'm Max, the butler, at your service.

Woof! I'm Spotless – aptly named, as you can see. I'm the family's loyal dog.

Contents

Young and Old

Sir Ralph and Isabella Witherbottom were on their way to see Isabella's grandma, with Max, the butler.

"How old is grandma?" asked Isabella. Sir Ralph had his eyes closed and replied sleepily, "I don't know. She was 29 when I was born and I'm now 52."

Isabella put her brain into gear. "29 add 52. Well... 20 add 50 is 70. 9 add 2 is 11. So 70 and 11 is 81. That makes grandma 81." Sir Ralph had drifted off to sleep and didn't hear this over his snoring, but Max had been listening.

"I use a different method," he said to Isabella. "I **round** 29 up to 30. Add together 30 and 52 to make 82 and then remember to take away 1 to make 81."

"That's a good method," Isabella replied. "How old are you, Max?"

"46 years young," Max responded, emphasising the word 'young'.

Isabella then tried to work out the **difference** in age between Max and Sir Ralph, but she could only picture it in her head as a written sum:

$$\begin{array}{r} 52 \\ - \ 46 \\ \hline \end{array}$$

This was too difficult for her to work out mentally, but once again Max had a better method.

"Imagine a number line in your head, with 46 at one end and 52 at the other end. Count on from 46 to 50, which is 4, and then on from 50 to 52, which is another 2. So the difference between 46 and 52 is 6."

"Fantastic," shouted Isabella, making Sir Ralph jump in his sleep. "So the difference between your age, 46, and grandma's, 81, is... 35 years."

"Isn't age a funny thing?" continued Isabella thoughtfully. "Dad looks more than 6 years older than you, but behaves much younger!"

Max looked in his rear-view mirror and pulled a face, sticking his tongue out at Isabella.

"OK," Isabella laughed, "you can be pretty childish too sometimes!"

46, but oh so handsome!

Top Tips!

There are many different mental methods for adding and subtracting numbers. Learn two or three of these methods and then look at the numbers involved to quickly work out which is the best method to use. For example, 101 – 89 is easy if you count on from 89.

Did you know?

Addition and subtraction are **inverse** or opposite **operations**, which is very useful for missing number problems. For example, if you can work out that 34 + 52 = 86, you can use this to work out any of these:

86 – ☐ = 34	86 – ☐ = 52	☐ – 34 = 52	☐ – 52 = 34

Use the two numbers that you have and add or subtract to find the missing number.

Your Number's Up

Isabella Witherbottom's school was running a talent show and Isabella had come up with a great idea. She decided to train Spotless to be the brainiest dog in Britain and answer times tables questions. She explained her plan to Sir Ralph Witherbottom.

"I'll write a set of numbers on a board and ask a question, such as 6 times 8, with Spotless standing next to me. When I point to each number I'll ask Spotless if this is the correct answer and when I point and say '48', Spotless will cleverly sit down!"

"Fantastic… How will he do that?" Sir Ralph wasn't convinced.

"Easy," replied Isabella. "I'll secretly click my fingers behind my back at the right moment. He always sits down when I click my fingers!"

Isabella spent the next 30 minutes practising until Spotless really did seem very clever.

$3 \times 9 = 27$, $8 \times 8 = 64$,

$7 \times 6 = 42$, $9 \times 8 = 72$,

$6 \times 4 = 24$, $9 \times 5 = 45$,

$4 \times 7 = 28$

For the talent show, Isabella was asked to design and print the family tickets, as a homework project.

"I like your design," said Sir Ralph, looking over her shoulder at the computer screen. "How many do you need to print?"

Isabella looked puzzled. "That's the tricky bit. All I know is that there are 8 rows, each with 30 seats, and that the family tickets are for 4 people."

Sir Ralph helped her. "So the total number of seats is

8 × 30. 8 × 3 is 24, so 8 × 30 is 240

As the family tickets are for 4 people, you need to divide this number by 4.

24 ÷ 4 is 6, so 240 ÷ 4 is 60

You need 60 tickets."

Max, the butler, walked in with an armful of clothes. "I've made Spotless an outfit so he looks suitably clever. What is your act going to be called?"

"Spotless: the Calculating Canine," replied Isabella. "If he wins the show, I'll get him to help me with my homework!"

Top Tips

Really knowing your tables and understanding **place value** are the keys to working out mental multiplication and division. If you know that 7 × 8 is 56 you can use this to help you with all of these:

70 × 8	0.7 × 8	70 × 80
7 × 0.8	0.7 × 0.8	700 × 8

Did you know?

These are ten of the trickiest tables facts, so learn these and the rest are easy! Remember, a tables fact can be read both ways round, so 3 × 8 has the same answer as 8 × 3.

3 × 8 = 24	4 × 7 = 28	4 × 8 = 32	4 × 9 = 36	6 × 7 = 42
6 × 8 = 48	6 × 9 = 54	7 × 8 = 56	7 × 9 = 63	8 × 9 = 72

Game Mania

Isabella had been saving her money to buy a new electronic game station. She already had £128 in the bank and she had saved £33.75 from her previous few months' pocket money. She was trying to add the amounts together in her head, with her eyes screwed up and her tongue poking out, when she was interrupted by a tap on her shoulder.

"Ahem...," coughed Max politely.
"Judging by the face you are pulling, I assume you are trying to work something out. Can I be of any assistance?"

Isabella explained her problem and Max showed her a good written method.

"Make sure you line up the columns and decimal points, one below the other, and then start adding the **digits** from the right. If the answer is larger than 9, include the tens digit in the next column." Max wrote it out on paper to show Isabella.

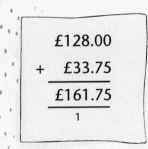

```
   £128.00
+   £33.75
─────────
  £161.75
        1
```

The next task was to work out the best deal for a game station. Isabella decided on the offer from 'GameMania' which had it priced at £146, with an extra handset at only £9.35.

```
   £146.00
+    £9.35
─────────
  £155.35
        1
```

"I'll get the other handset so you can play as well, Max," laughed Isabella.

Sir Ralph wasn't impressed when he heard Isabella and Max talking about the game station.

I'll just have a quick go, whilst no-one's around...

"Waste of money, those things, and you'll end up with thumbs twice as strong as they should be! And Max... you'll be too busy to waste your time playing these games, surely?"

Isabella disagreed. "It's very educational. I can now do a written method of adding, which I might not have learnt if I hadn't been buying it!" she replied smugly.

Top Tips

Always quickly **estimate** an **approximate** answer when you're adding large numbers or decimals. Once you've finished the addition, check that it is close to your estimate. If it isn't close, double-check each column for any errors.

Did you know?

Here is a method to work out the sum of **consecutive numbers**. For example, from 5 to 11 (5 + 6 + 7 + 8 + 9 + 10 + 11):

1 Add the start and end numbers: 5 + 11 = 16
2 Find the difference between these numbers and add 1: (11 − 5) + 1 = 7
3 Multiply the two numbers together and divide by 2: 7 × 16 ÷ 2
   (the same as 7 × 8)

So the sum of the numbers from 5 to 11 is 56. Try this with other consecutive numbers.

Take-Away Troubles

Isabella was using Sir Ralph's whiteboard for her homework.

Sir Ralph was interested in the method she was using to work out 873 – 145.

"I count on from 145 to 200, which is 55, then from 200 to 873, which is 673. Then add together 673 and 55, which is... 728," explained Isabella.

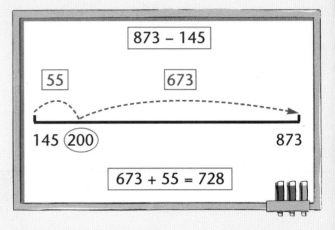

"Not bad, but why not try the method I use?" replied Sir Ralph.

"Notice how I make 73 into 60 and 13 so that I can take away the 5 from the 13. This is called decomposition. Try it yourself."

```
      6  1
    8 X 3
  – 1 4 5
   ‾‾‾‾‾‾‾
    7 2 8
```

Isabella hadn't listened carefully because she knew her TV programme started in 5 minutes. She quickly answered the next two questions and closed her book. Sir Ralph was amazed; even he couldn't complete them that quickly. He opened the book – what a mess!

```
    4 9 2          5 7 9
  – 2 6 4        – 3 3 7
   ‾‾‾‾‾‾         ‾‾‾‾‾‾
    2 3 2          3 2 0 9
```

Sir Ralph was disappointed. "I'll have to 'take away' your TV time until these are corrected."

Isabella felt she had let her father down by not listening carefully, so she tried hard this time. Sir Ralph noticed that Isabella was sorry, so he winked at Max, who then slipped away quietly and recorded the programme for her.

Max passed a note to Sir Ralph, 'programme recorded'. Sir Ralph smiled and checked Isabella's work. It was all correct, so Sir Ralph announced that she could watch her programme as Max had kindly recorded it. He then added that as an extra treat they would all have a different kind of take-away – no cooking for Max tonight!

This is my kind of take-away.

Top Tips

The 'number line' method and decomposition are two good ways to subtract numbers on paper. Practise both methods to see which you prefer. Which is the quickest method? Which is the neatest method? Most importantly, which method do you find is the easiest way to get correct answers?

Did you know?

You don't always need to use a written method if you are subtracting with big numbers. Working it out in your head can be easier and quicker. Look at the numbers and see if you can work the answer out mentally. For example, 7002 – 6997 could be tricky on paper, but counting on in your head to find the difference between the two numbers is easy.

Driving to the Moon

Isabella had returned home after a tiring but enjoyable school trip to the Planetarium in London. She was telling Sir Ralph about an interesting fact they'd been told that day – that the distance from the earth to the moon is 600 times longer than their coach journey from school to the Planetarium and back again.

"The bus driver said we travelled 640km today, but I can't work out how to make this 600 times bigger."

"No problem, Izzy. Let me show you my excellent column method. First thing to notice – if you are multiplying a number by 600, it is the same as multiplying by 6 and then making the answer 100 times bigger. Always look at the numbers to try to make it simpler."

Column Method

$$640 \times 600$$

$$
\begin{array}{r}
640 \\
\times \quad 6 \\
\hline
3840 \\
\end{array}
$$
$\;_2$

$\times 100 = 384{,}000$km

One small step for man, one giant leap for mankind... one long journey for me!

"Keep the numbers in line and then remember to multiply 3840 by 100. So the distance to the moon is 384,000km."

Sir Ralph looked thoughtful and let his mind wander. "I wonder how long it would take? Well, if I drove to London and back every day for 600 days I would drive the same distance as to the moon. There are 365 days in a year and 365 multiplied by 2 is well over 600, so it would take less than 2 years."

Max walked into the room and saw Sir Ralph's column method. He explained that he preferred using the grid method, "especially if you're an untidy mathematician," he added, with a sideways look at Sir Ralph. "You need to break the numbers into hundreds, tens and ones and multiply each part."

Sir Ralph agreed and added, "Yes, I like that method, Max. It also works well with 2-digit numbers."

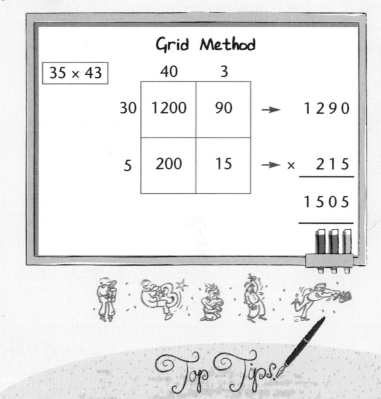

Grid Method

35×43	40	3
30	1200	90
5	200	15

→ 1290
→ × 215

1505

Top Tips!

When multiplying large numbers or decimals, more errors are made by getting the **place value** wrong than by making mistakes with multiplication facts. Always double-check the value of the numbers you are multiplying and check that the answer makes sense.

Did you know?

Before calculators, people used many different methods to help multiply large numbers together. In 1617 the Scotsman John Napier invented 'Napier's Bones' which were calculating rods made from wood or ivory. They made multiplication easier by changing the calculation to an addition. Search for 'Napier's Bones' on the Internet to find out how they work.

Blankets and Nets

Sir Ralph had received an email from an old friend, Sir Rodney, who was off travelling round the world. He was in a village that had been hit by a small earthquake a year ago. Most things had returned to normal, but they were still in need of blankets and mosquito nets. He asked if Sir Ralph could help by sending supplies to the village.

Sir Ralph, Max and Isabella set to work immediately. Isabella searched on the Internet for the best place to buy blankets and nets, and found blankets in packs of 14 and mosquito nets in packs of 8. Max found out from Sir Rodney's email that there were 336 people that needed these supplies and he calculated how many packs of each were needed.

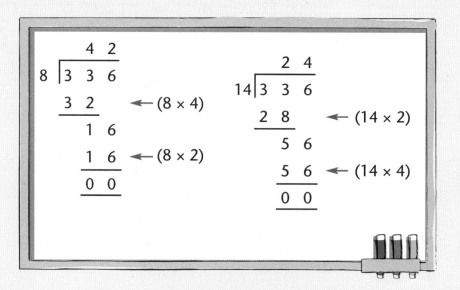

So they needed to order 42 packs of mosquito nets and 24 packs of blankets. Sir Ralph found that the box for shipping them over still had room for some small things, so he suggested the school might welcome some pencils for the classrooms. Isabella emailed Sir Rodney for more information. He replied that there were 176 children in the school. Pencils were packed in boxes of 6 and she wanted to send enough pencils for there to be one for each child.

Isabella tried a shorter written method than her father's to divide 176 by 6.

$$6 \overline{)1\ 7_5\ 6} = 2\ 9\ r\ 2$$

That extra pack of pencils is really weighing this down!

She was about to order 29 boxes of pencils when she was interrupted by a discreet cough from Max. "If you send 29 packs there won't be enough for every child to have a pencil. They would need two more. If you send 30 packs there will be four pencils left over; just enough for each of the teachers!"

Top Tips!

You can use multiplication as 'lots of' to help you with long division. For example, '72 divided by 12 makes 6' can be worked out as '6 lots of 12 make 72'. Write down the multiplication for each step and double-check that the division is correct.

Did you know?

Divisions on a calculator may produce a decimal answer rather than a remainder. For example, $384 \div 7 = 54.857142$. With real problems this may not be very helpful, so use multiplication to work out the whole number remainder.

$54 \times 7 = 378$, so the remainder is $384 - 378 = 6$.

Counting Coins

Max was helping Isabella at the school fête. As she enjoyed maths, she had been asked to count the money raised by each stall. Throughout the afternoon, they counted coins and wrote down all the totals.

Raffle	Tombola	Hook-the-duck	Whack-the-rat	Cake stall
£134	£28	£21	£15	£37

They had just finished counting when the head teacher asked them approximately how much money there was in total. Max quickly replied that there was about £240, before Isabella had even had a chance to add up the raffle and tombola money. The head teacher left to announce the amount raised and to draw the raffle. Isabella asked Max how he had added the totals up so quickly. He explained that he had **rounded** each amount to the nearest ten, making them easier to add. He showed Isabella:

Raffle	Tombola	Hook-the-duck	Whack-the-rat	Cake stall
£134 → £130	£28 → £30	£21 → £20	£15 → £20	£37 → £40

Max explained. "Look at the ones digit. If it is less than 5, round down so the tens digit stays the same. If it is 5 or more, round up to the next ten. Add them all up: £130 + £30 + £20 + £20 + £40 = £240."

Max then explained that decimals can be rounded to whole numbers in a similar way –

"£3.20, £3.47 and £3.09 all round down to £3, and £3.58, £3.70 and £3.83 all round up to £4."

The ice-cream stall was still open so Max gave Isabella some change and asked her to buy 3 ice-creams. The ice-creams cost £1.20 each and Max explained that he had given her approximately the right amount of money by rounding each price to the nearest £1. Isabella was halfway to the stall when she realised that Max had tricked her. Rounding down meant that there wasn't enough money. Using rounding can be helpful, but using common sense is essential, as Izzy had found out – the hard way!

I've rounded off the top of this ice-cream, to the nearest hundreds and thousands!

Top Tips

Remember that a number always lies between two possible 'round' numbers – you just have to choose which one it's nearest to. Picture it on a number line – anything halfway and beyond rounds up. This rule applies to rounding to the nearest whole number, ten, hundred or thousand. For example, 781, to the nearest hundred, rounds up to 800.

781

750

700   800

Rounds down   Rounds up

Did you know?

The sign ≈ means 'is approximately equal to'. **Approximate** numbers are often used in newspaper headlines so that they are easier to read, particularly with large numbers. So, for example, if £5,031,900 was raised for famine relief, the headline could read: '£5 million pledged for famine aid'.

Mobile Madness

Isabella was buying a mobile phone, but she couldn't work out the cheaper offer:

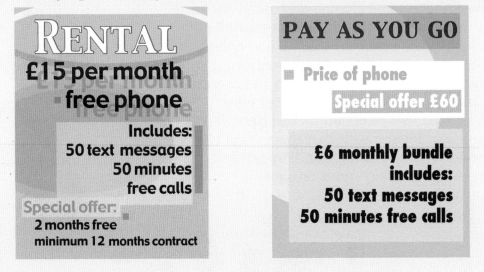

RENTAL

£15 per month
free phone

Includes:
50 text messages
50 minutes
free calls

Special offer:
2 months free
minimum 12 months contract

PAY AS YOU GO

Price of phone
Special offer £60

£6 monthly bundle
includes:
50 text messages
50 minutes free calls

She was in a muddle, so she showed her calculations to Sir Ralph.

"For the rented phone, I multiplied £15 × 12 for the cost in a year, which came to £180," she explained. "For the 'pay as you go' phone, the total for a year came to £792! I added together £60 and £6 and multiplied this by 12 to find the total for a year. This can't be right though – what have I done wrong?"

Sir Ralph spotted the problems straight away. "Brackets may be useful here," he explained.

Rental	Pay as you go
£15 each month, 2 months free	£60 + £6 a month
(12 – 2) × £15 =	£60 + (£6 × 12) =
10 × 15 = £150	60 + 72 = £132

"For the rented phone you forgot to take away the two free months. For the 'pay as you go' phone you only pay for the phone once and then the £6 bundle needs to be bought each month. If you don't use brackets you get a completely different answer."

$$60 + 6 \times 12 = 792 \qquad 60 + (6 \times 12) = 132$$

Isabella worked out the costs again, remembering to work out the bit in the brackets first. She realised that the 'pay as you go' phone would save her £18 in a year.

Max overheard the conversation and added, "You will save even more if you keep the phone for two years. The rented phone is still £15 a month, whereas the 'pay as you go' phone is only £6 a month for the bundle."

Isabella smiled. "Well, I don't need to 'phone a friend' to see which is the cheaper offer now!"

Top Tips

Use these four steps to solve problems:
1 Read the problem – *What is it asking?*
2 Sort out the calculations – *Be organised*
3 Answer the calculations – *No silly errors*
4 Look back at the problem – *Have you answered it?*

Did you know?

You may have heard of BODMAS. It is an acronym – which means the letters of the word stand for other words:

Brackets Of Division Multiplication Addition Subtraction
('Of' actually means 'power of', as in 3^2.

BODMAS shows the *order* of calculating equations, i.e which part of a calculation you should work out first.

For example:

$(4 + 2) \times 3^2 - 10$	Brackets first
$6 \times 3^2 - 10$	Of – work out any powers next
$6 \times 9 - 10$	Multiplication next
$54 - 10$	Subtract to finish
$= 44$	

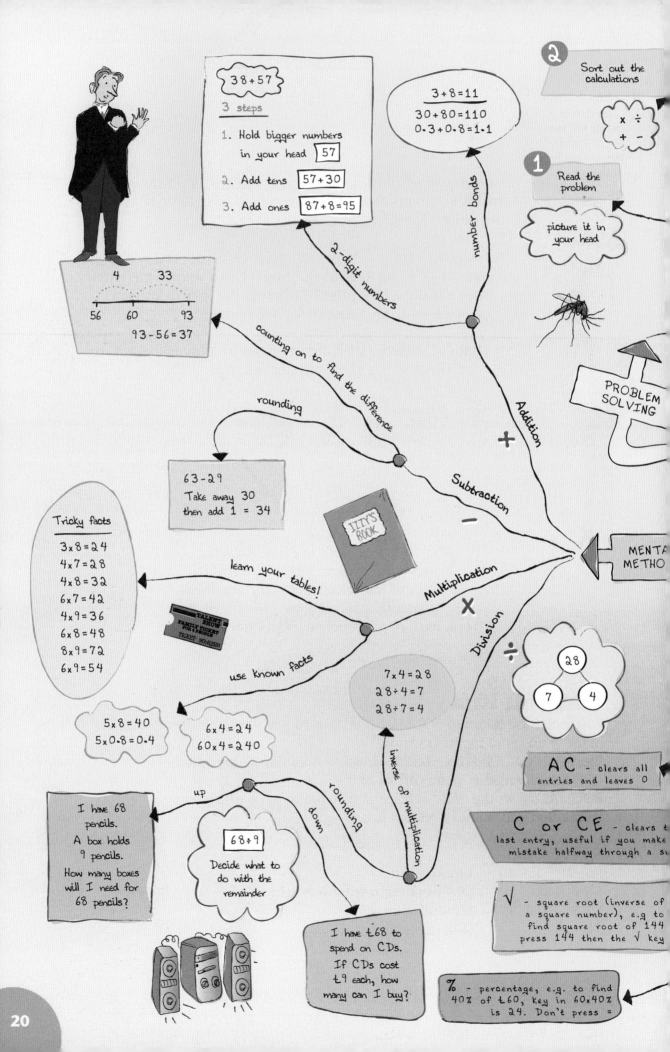

$38 + 57$

3 steps

1. Hold bigger numbers in your head $\boxed{57}$
2. Add tens $\boxed{57 + 30}$
3. Add ones $\boxed{87 + 8 = 95}$

$3 + 8 = 11$
$30 + 80 = 110$
$0.3 + 0.8 = 1.1$

number bonds

2-digit numbers

4   33

56   60   93

$93 - 56 = 37$

counting on to find the difference

rounding

$63 - 29$
Take away 30
then add 1 = 34

Sort out the calculations

x   ÷
+   −

Read the problem

picture it in your head

PROBLEM SOLVING

Addition
+

Subtraction
−

MENTAL METHOD

Tricky facts

$3 \times 8 = 24$
$4 \times 7 = 28$
$4 \times 8 = 32$
$6 \times 7 = 42$
$4 \times 9 = 36$
$6 \times 8 = 48$
$8 \times 9 = 72$
$6 \times 9 = 54$

learn your tables!

ITZY'S BOOK

Multiplication
×

TALENT SHOW
FAMILY TICKET
FOR 4 PEOPLE
TICKET NO: 412551

use known facts

$7 \times 4 = 28$
$28 \div 4 = 7$
$28 \div 7 = 4$

Division
÷

28

7   4

$5 \times 8 = 40$
$5 \times 0.8 = 0.4$

$6 \times 4 = 24$
$60 \times 4 = 240$

AC - clears all entries and leaves 0

up

I have 68 pencils.
A box holds 9 pencils.
How many boxes will I need for 68 pencils?

$68 \div 9$

Decide what to do with the remainder

down

rounding

inverse of multiplication

C or CE - clears the last entry, useful if you make a mistake halfway through a su

√ - square root (inverse of a square number), e.g to find square root of 144 press 144 then the √ key

I have £68 to spend on CDs.
If CDs cost £9 each, how many can I buy?

% - percentage, e.g. to find 40% of £60, key in 60×40% is 24. Don't press =

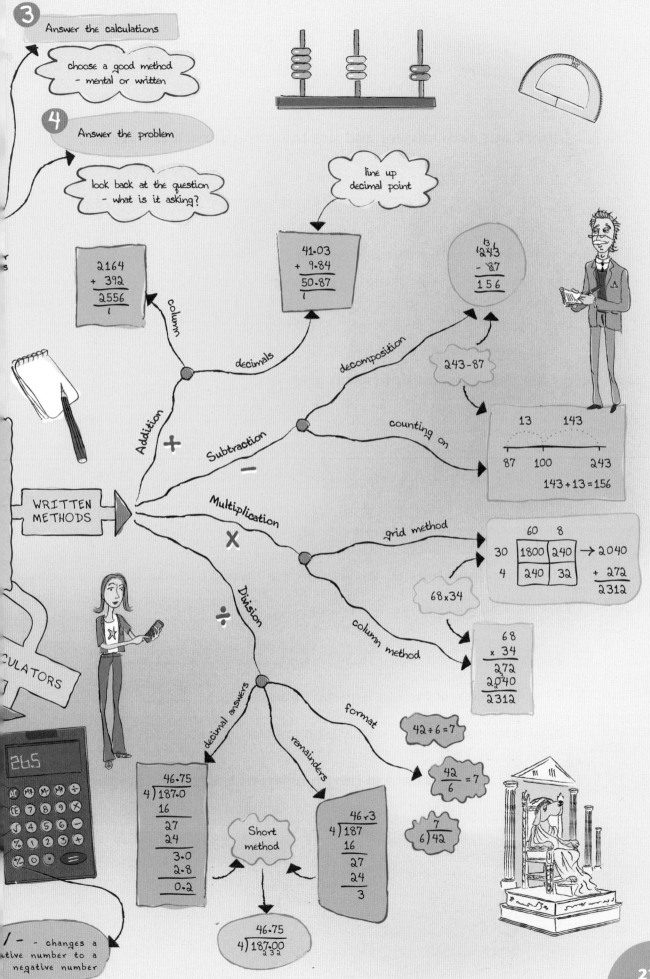

3 Answer the calculations

choose a good method
- mental or written

4 Answer the problem

look back at the question
- what is it asking?

line up
decimal point

WRITTEN
METHODS

Addition +

column

2164
+ 392
2556
1

decimals

41·03
+ 9·84
50·87
1

Subtraction −

decomposition

13
1243
- 87
156

243-87

counting on

13   143
87 100   243
143 + 13 = 156

Multiplication ×

grid method

    60   8
30 1800 240 → 2040
4   240   32   + 272
                  2312

68 x 34

column method

  68
× 34
 272
2340
2312

Division ÷

decimal answers

  46·75
4)187·0
  16
  27
  24
  3·0
  2·8
  0·2

remainders

  46 r 3
4)187
  16
  27
  24
   3

Short method

  46·75
4)187·00

format

42 ÷ 6 = 7

42/6 = 7

7
6)42

CALCULATORS

265

/ − - changes a
[posi]tive number to a
negative number

21

Revise Time

1 Work out each answer and use the grid to crack the code.

38	27	29	52	65	83
P	B	T	N	O	A

You are a...

$74 - 45$ $36 + 29$ $66 - 28$

= [ ] = [65] = [38]

$54 - 27$ $64 + 19$ $98 - 46$ $39 + 44$ $80 - 28$ $58 + 25$

= [ ] = [ ] = [ ] = [ ] = [ ] = [ ]

2 Complete this multiplication grid.

×	6	8	9	3
9	54	72	81	27
7	42	56		21
4	24	32	36	12
5	30	40	45	15

3 Use these numbers to answer the following questions.

59.8   17.24   106.48   28.6   83.72   119.3

a Which two numbers total 136.54? _____ _____

b What is the sum of the two largest numbers? _____

c What is the sum of the two smallest numbers? _____

4 What is the difference in length between these three lengths of wood?

a 3.27m   **b** 1.89m   **c** 0.91m

a a − b = [ ]   b a − c = [ ]   c b − c = [ ]

5 Work out the answers to these clues and complete the puzzle.

Across

2 27 × 26

4 261 × 3

5 29 × 31

6 199 × 3

Down

1 34 × 25

2 49 × 15

3 41 × 7

7 53 × 18

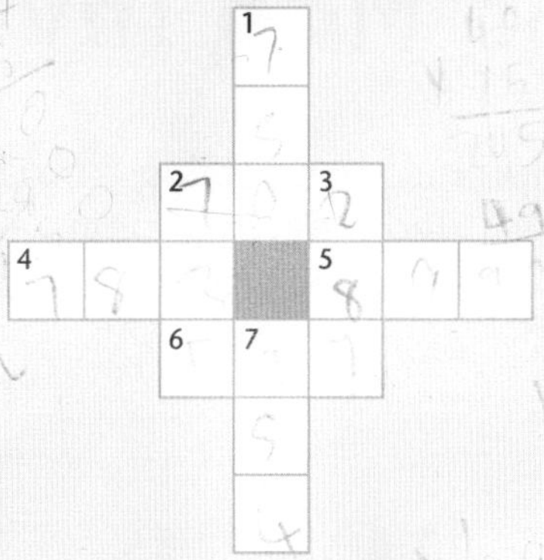

6 Use each digit to complete these.

| 1 | 2 | 3 | 4 | 5 | 6 |

a
```
      4 2
   ┌──────
 3 │ 1 2 6
```

b
```
      1 7 3
   ┌────────
 5 │ 8 86 5
```

c
```
      1 9 6
   ┌────────
 8 │ 7 6 8
```

7 Circle three items that have an approximate total of £100.

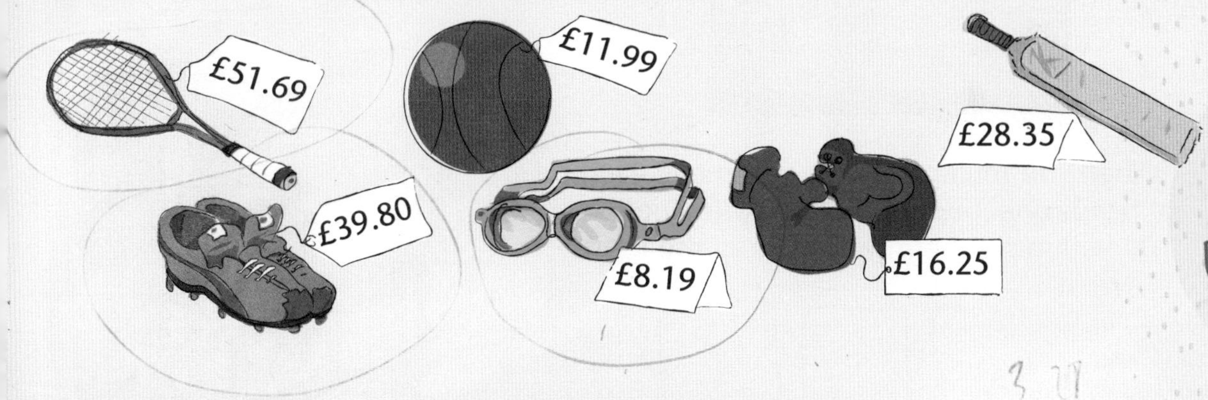

£51.69

£11.99

£28.35

£39.80

£8.19

£16.25

8 Draw brackets to make these calculations correct.

a 9 – 4 + 3 = 2

b 24 ÷ 3 × 4 = 32

c 7 × 4 – 3 + 6 = 19

d 18 – 2 × 4 + 2 = 96

The Mad Inventor

Sir Ralph had been trying for days to invent a new **abacus**. He wanted an abacus that included a decimal point and would help to multiply or divide by 10 or 100. He showed Isabella how a normal abacus worked.

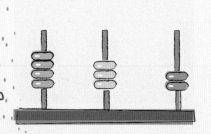

"This shows 4 hundreds, 3 tens and 2 ones. 400 + 30 + 2, which is 432," explained Sir Ralph. "What I can't easily show is how to make that number 10 or 100 times bigger or smaller."

Isabella was only half listening though, as she was concentrating on her 'Buzzer Game'. She had to keep her hand steady so the hoop didn't touch the bent wire, which she was finding very tricky. Sir Ralph jumped when the buzzer rudely interrupted his thoughts, but rather than being angry, he leapt up and clapped his hands. "That's it!" he shouted, rushing out of the room.

Later in the day, Sir Ralph produced his new abacus and explained how it worked.

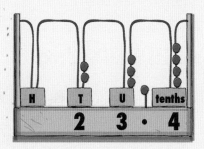

H	T	U	tenths
	2	3 ·	4

"When you multiply by 10, you move each set of beads one loop to the left. To multiply by 100 you move them two loops to the left."

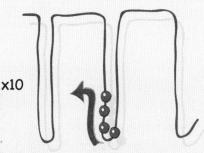

x10

How do you turn this thing off?!

"When you divide by 10 you move each set of beads one loop to the right. To divide by 100 you move them two loops to the right."

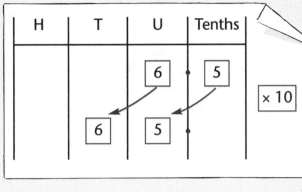

H	T	U	Tenths
		6 ·	5
	6	5 ·	

× 10

Isabella thought the abacus was very clever, but she knew it wouldn't catch on, mostly because she knew that to multiply a number by 10 or 100 you just moved the digits to the left. They had used digit cards at school to show this.

Sir Ralph was thrilled with his latest invention. "Now all it needs are some flashing lights and buzzers to make it a bit more exciting. Teachers will love it!"

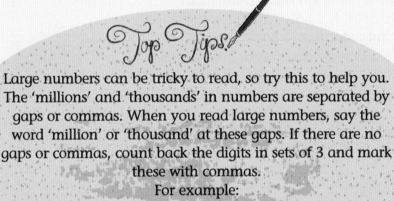

Top Tips!

Large numbers can be tricky to read, so try this to help you. The 'millions' and 'thousands' in numbers are separated by gaps or commas. When you read large numbers, say the word 'million' or 'thousand' at these gaps. If there are no gaps or commas, count back the digits in sets of 3 and mark these with commas.
For example:
387,910 → three hundred and eighty-seven thousand, nine hundred and ten
2,436,500 → two million, four hundred and thirty-six thousand, five hundred

Did you know?

The Soroban is an abacus that is used widely in Japan and around the world. With practice it can be used very quickly to make numbers and to calculate mentally. It is laid flat and the four beads at the bottom have a 'one' value and the single beads at the top have a 'five' value. This number shows 275. See if you can work out what the number 1648 would look like.

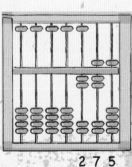

2 7 5

Dog-Day Afternoon

It was the day of the Fun Dog Show and Isabella had entered Spotless into three competitions. The judges awarded marks out of 10 for each round and added them up to find the winner. In the 'Waggiest Tail' competition Spotless scored 8.4. Isabella wrote down the scores for each of the dogs to try to put them in order:

Spotless	Pat	Growler	K-9	Hairy
8.4	8.15	8.2	8.35	8.05

I think my knobbly knees might let us down in this one, Spotless!

BEST 6 LEGS COMPETITION

Sir Ralph looked at the scores and saw that Spotless was in the lead, which confused Isabella as she thought K-9 was winning with 8.35. Sir Ralph realised what she was doing wrong. "When you compare decimal numbers, look at the whole numbers first, then the tenths and then the hundredths. 8.4 and 8.35 have the same whole numbers, but 8.4 has 4 tenths, whereas 8.35 has only 3 tenths and 5 hundredths."

Isabella now understood and so put the scores in order:

Spotless	K-9	Growler	Pat	Hairy
8.4	8.35	8.2	8.15	8.05

The next competition was an obedience test. Spotless wasn't quite as good at this, preferring to jump about rather than walk to heel or lie down, but he did sit and stay very well. These were the scores in order:

Hairy	K-9	Growler	Spotless	Pat
6.12	6.1	6	5.84	5.52

Isabella realised that 6 is 6.00 and 6.1 is 6.10. Once they all had 2 decimal places it was easier to put the scores in order.

The final competition was the obstacle course. Spotless loved jumping through hoops and walking in and out of poles!

These were the scores in order:

Growler	Pat	Spotless	Hairy	K-9
9.13	9.08	8.96	8.91	8.72

The total scores were announced in reverse order, with loud applause for each dog.

"In fifth place is Pat the dog, with 22.75 points. In fourth place, with 23.08 points, is Hairy. In third place is K-9, with 23.17 points. Runner up, with 23.2 points, is Spotless, and the winner, with 23.33 points, is Growler!"

What a great day, and Spotless looked really pleased with his huge 2nd place rosette!

Top Tips

Follow these four easy steps to order decimals:
1 Write them out one under the other, lining up the decimal points.
2 Compare the digits from the left-hand side to the right-hand side.
3 Look for the smallest digit and write this number in a separate list. If the digits are the same, compare the next digit to the right.
4 Keep comparing the numbers in this way until all the numbers are written out in order.

Did you know?

When you compare numbers, you may be asked to use these signs: < and >.
< means 'is less than'
i.e. 7.4 < 7.9
> means 'is greater than'
i.e. 3.4 > 3.12
Remember – the bigger number is at the open end.

Dreadful Drawers

Sir Ralph was sorting his files out and asked Isabella to draw diagrams of all the cabinets, shading in the full drawers. He wanted to work out what fraction of each cabinet was full.

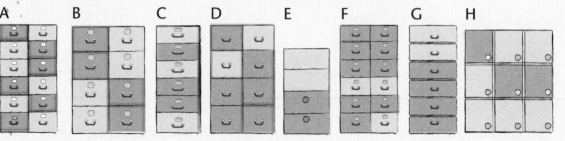

A   B   C   D   E   F   G   H

Isabella wrote down the number of full drawers out of the total number of drawers in each cabinet. For example, in one cabinet, 2 out of 4 drawers were full, so she wrote $\frac{2}{4}$.

Sir Ralph looked at Isabella's work. "Oh good, there are a few that are only half full. Could you mark those so that I can fill them up?"

Isabella was confused as she hadn't found any that were $\frac{1}{2}$. Then she looked more carefully. She could see that E was half full, but her fraction said $\frac{2}{4}$, not $\frac{1}{2}$. Then it clicked: **equivalent fractions**! She saw a pattern with the numbers: the **numerator** is exactly half of the **denominator**. She looked for other fractions with the same pattern.

$\frac{2}{4}$ → 2 is half of 4	$\frac{6}{12}$ → 6 is half of 12
$\frac{4}{8}$ → 4 is half of 8	$\frac{3}{6}$ → 3 is half of 6

> *Reducing fractions is easy... I wish it was as easy to reduce paperwork!*

Isabella checked with Max that these all equalled $\frac{1}{2}$. He agreed that they did, but said there was another way to find equivalent fractions.

"$\frac{2}{4}$ can be reduced to $\frac{1}{2}$ by dividing both the numerator and denominator by 2," he explained. He then showed this method for the other fractions.

$\frac{6}{12}$ → divide top and bottom by 6 → $\frac{1}{2}$

$\frac{4}{8}$ → divide top and bottom by 4 → $\frac{1}{2}$

$\frac{3}{6}$ → divide top and bottom by 3 → $\frac{1}{2}$

Max explained that this was called, 'reducing a fraction to its lowest terms'.

They looked at the filing cabinets that remained.

"$\frac{3}{9}$ is easy to simplify. 9 and 3 can both be divided by 3, so it is reduced to $\frac{1}{3}$."
Max continued. "$\frac{6}{8}$ is a bit trickier. Can you work it out?"

$\frac{3}{9}$ → divide top and bottom by 3 → $\frac{1}{3}$

$\frac{6}{8}$ → divide top and bottom by 2 → $\frac{3}{4}$

$\frac{9}{12}$ → divide top and bottom by 3 → $\frac{3}{4}$

"6 divided by 2 is 3, and 8 divided by 2 is 4, so $\frac{6}{8}$ is the same as $\frac{3}{4}$," replied Isabella. "I can see that $\frac{9}{12}$ is also $\frac{3}{4}$, by dividing the top and bottom by 3."

They worked out that $\frac{4}{6} = \frac{2}{3}$ in the same way, dividing the numerator and denominator by 2.

Top Tips

The bottom number of a fraction is called the denominator and shows the number of equal parts. The top number is called the numerator and shows how many of the parts are taken.

This shows $\frac{1}{6}$. There are six equal parts. 1 part is taken.

This shows $\frac{5}{6}$. There are six equal parts. 5 parts are taken.

Did you know?

Tangrams are Chinese puzzles that involve arranging the 7 pieces to make shapes. Each piece is a fraction of the whole square. For example, each large triangle is $\frac{1}{4}$ of the square. It can be used to explore different fractions and shapes.

Hats and Horses

Isabella was helping out at the riding stables. She helped clean out the stables and then led the horses out, ready for the riders in the next lesson. She then went to the shed where her job was to line up all the riding hats in size order. The numbers inside the hats had fractions and Isabella didn't quite know where to start.

The hats showed: $6\frac{3}{8}$, $6\frac{7}{8}$, $6\frac{3}{4}$, $6\frac{1}{2}$, $6\frac{5}{8}$, $6\frac{1}{8}$, $6\frac{1}{4}$

Some she already knew and lined up, starting with the smallest:

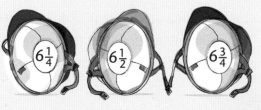

$6\frac{1}{4}$, $6\frac{1}{2}$, $6\frac{3}{4}$

She noticed that the ones left all had the same **denominator**: 8. That made things easy as she could order the **numerators**:

$6\frac{1}{8}$, $6\frac{3}{8}$, $6\frac{5}{8}$, $6\frac{7}{8}$

She now needed to put them together. She could work out that $\frac{1}{8}$ was smaller than $\frac{1}{4}$. She pictured a pie cut into 4 pieces and another in to 8 pieces to help her:

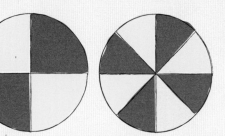

Thinking of the pie gave her an idea. She could see that $\frac{1}{4}$ was equivalent to $\frac{2}{8}$ so she decided to change all the fractions into eighths:

$$6\frac{1}{4} = 6\frac{2}{8} \qquad 6\frac{1}{2} = 6\frac{4}{8} \qquad 6\frac{3}{4} = 6\frac{6}{8}$$

Now it was easy to put them all in order:

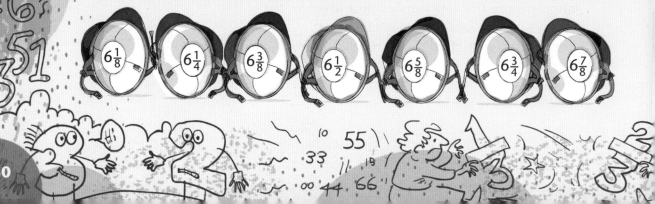

$6\frac{1}{8}$, $6\frac{1}{4}$, $6\frac{3}{8}$, $6\frac{1}{2}$, $6\frac{5}{8}$, $6\frac{3}{4}$, $6\frac{7}{8}$

When Isabella got home she looked in Sir Ralph's, riding hat. It was size $7\frac{7}{8}$! Max explained that this was the biggest hat size you could get.

"A big head is needed for such a large brain," added Sir Ralph, smiling. Isabella pointed out that it looked as if it hadn't been worn for years.

Sir Ralph looked a bit flustered. "Well, riding a horse is just like riding a bike. Once you learn, you never forget."

Never could ride a bike...

Top Tips

If you are comparing two fractions to see which is bigger, you can change them so that they both have the same denominator or you can draw equivalence strips for each. Which is bigger; $\frac{3}{5}$ or $\frac{2}{3}$?
Make sure the strips are the same length, then divide them to match the denominators and shade them to compare the fractions.

$\frac{2}{3}$

$\frac{3}{5}$

Did you know?

You can change a fraction to an equivalent decimal and then put the decimals in order. If you are allowed to use a calculator for your test, it is simple to change a fraction to a decimal. Just use the line as a division sign. For example, $\frac{3}{8} = 3 \div 8 = 0.375$

Who Ate All the Pies?

*½ apple,
⅓ raspberry,
⅙ apricot.*

Max was a marvellous cook – well, a lot better than Sir Ralph anyway! Today he had decided to bake 24 small fruit pies. Isabella liked to help with the eating, particularly her favourites – apricot.

"What would you prefer, Izzy?" asked Max. "You can have all the apricot pies, or you can share 24 equally with Sir Ralph and myself and we'll each have $\frac{1}{3}$."

Isabella thought for a moment. First she worked out how many apricot pies there were.

"$\frac{1}{6}$ are apricot," she thought, "which means 6 equal parts. So divide 24 by 6, which is 4 apricot pies."

She then needed to work out how many pies she would have if she had $\frac{1}{3}$ of them. "24 divided by 3 is 8 pies," she calculated.

"I know what I want," Isabella exclaimed. "I would like $\frac{1}{3}$ of the pies, but I would like half of them to be apricot!"

"Very clever, although a little greedy," Max replied, with a smile.

Suddenly Isabella jumped up. "I nearly forgot – my three friends are coming over today and they'll want some pies!"

Max paused and rubbed his chin. "I want to keep $\frac{1}{3}$ of the pies, so I can let you and your friends have $\frac{2}{3}$. Will that be enough?"

Isabella knew that $\frac{1}{3}$ of 24 was 8, but what about $\frac{2}{3}$?

$\frac{1}{3}$

$\frac{2}{3}$

"If $\frac{1}{3}$ of 24 is 8, then $\frac{2}{3}$ will be twice as many," she thought aloud. "That's it! You multiply by the **numerator**: 8 times 2 is 16. There will be 16 pies, which is plenty for the four of us." Max was putting $\frac{1}{3}$ of the pies into a tin when the doorbell rang.

"Must hide these or they'll eat the lot," Max muttered to Spotless, who had just walked into the kitchen. He then quickly went to the front door to welcome the visitors.

Isabella and her friends went into the kitchen and opened the tin on the table. Isabella turned to Max reproachfully.

"Why have you only left 8 for us? That's only $\frac{1}{3}$."

"They're the ones I'm keeping," he replied. "Your pies are still on the table."

Isabella looked at the empty plate on the table. There were a lot of crumbs and…. "SPOTLESS!" she shouted at the end of the tail disappearing round the door.

Phew! Got away with it… by a fraction!

Top Tips!

To work out fractions of amounts, divide by the **denominator** and then multiply by the numerator.
$\frac{3}{5}$ of 45 = 27 → 45 ÷ 5 = 9
9 × 3 = 27

Did you know?

You can change a fraction to an equivalent decimal. This is useful if a question allows you to use a calculator. Then the word 'of' in these fraction questions can mean 'multiplied by':
What is $\frac{2}{5}$ of £75? $\frac{2}{5}$ is the same as 2 ÷ 5, which is 0.4   0.4 × 75 = £30

Jungle Paint

Isabella wanted to decorate her room and had decided on a jungle theme, with green paint to match the curtains. Sir Ralph had lots of pots of paint in the shed, but there was no green. Fortunately there was a huge quantity of blue and yellow paint.

Isabella went to the shed in old clothes and began to experiment. She used a cup and mixed different **ratios** of blue to yellow to make different shades of green.

2 blue
1 yellow
2:1

1 blue
1 yellow
1:1

1 blue
2 yellow
1:2

3 blue
1 yellow
3:1

1 blue
3 yellow
1:3

As she mixed them, Max wrote down the ratio, showing the number of blue cups to yellow cups.

Isabella liked 1 cup of blue to 3 cups of yellow, as it made a bright green. Max agreed and starting mixing the paint, pouring in two pots of blue paint. Isabella thought he had made a mistake, because the ratio was 1:3.

Max explained that he needed a lot of paint, so he was increasing the amount but still keeping the same ratio. "So if I have 2 cupfuls of blue, how much yellow will I need?"

Isabella looked at the paint and spotted the pattern quickly. "If the ratio is 1:3, 2 pots of blue would need 6 pots of yellow. 1:3 is the same as 2:6 and the same as 3:9."

Just think what I could do with a paintbrush!

Isabella wanted to paint her own room border. She laid the strip out on the floor and was about to paint it as zebra stripes when Spotless walked along the border and left a fantastic paw-print pattern! He had put one paw in yellow paint and the other three paws in blue paint. Max showed that this could help explain **proportion**.

"Spotless made 4 prints. $\frac{1}{4}$ of them are yellow and $\frac{3}{4}$ are blue. So even if he makes 40 prints, the proportion of yellow prints is still $\frac{1}{4}$ of the whole amount."

Top Tips!

Don't muddle up ratio and proportion.
Proportion means the fraction of the whole amount. Count the total of all the items and work out the fraction:

The proportion of parrots that are green is $\frac{1}{3}$.
Ratio compares two sets. Count the total of the two sets being compared. The ratio of yellow to red parrots is 1:3.

Did you know?

Paper is mainly sold in sizes A0, A1, A2, A3, A4 up to A10. A4 is the usual photocopying size. The ratio of width to length of each size is 1 : 1.4
You could check this by measuring the paper.

Fun in the Lab

Isabella was flicking through an old book of experiments in Sir Ralph's laboratory when Max came rushing in, carrying a bag of frozen peas. The freezer had broken and he couldn't think of a way to keep the food frozen until the freezer was fixed.

"This book has something about making a chemical reaction to absorb heat," said Isabella, as she flicked through the pages. Max looked impressed, without really knowing what she was talking about.

"Here it is. If you want to make ice even colder, mix together $\frac{1}{5}$kg salt and $1\frac{3}{4}$kg crushed ice."

Max immediately went into action, getting ice, salt, some weighing scales and an ice crusher. Isabella weighed the salt, but couldn't work out how much $\frac{1}{5}$kg was on the scales.

Max explained that each kilogram is divided into hundredths. "These are the small markers, and then each tenth is numbered. So 0.1 is $\frac{1}{10}$, 0.2 is $\frac{2}{10}$, 0.3 is $\frac{3}{10}$ and so on. $\frac{2}{10}$ is equivalent to $\frac{1}{5}$, which means 0.2kg is the same as $\frac{1}{5}$kg."

Isabella listened carefully. "So each one of the small markers is 10g, and 0.1kg is actually 100g. We need 200g of salt. That sounds like a lot."

Max agreed that it was a lot of salt, but added that they were using a lot more ice. He showed Isabella that $\frac{1}{4}$kg is the same as 0.25kg and $\frac{3}{4}$kg is 0.75kg. "This means that $1\frac{3}{4}$kg of ice is the same as 1.75kg, or 1kg 750g," he explained.

They crushed and weighed the ice and added the salt, giving it a stir and putting the mixture into an old bath. They needed to repeat this three times to make enough ice to freeze all the pizzas, ice-cream and fish fingers that Sir Ralph secretly loved!

Professor Izzy Einstein, discovering relatively little!

Top Tips!

A decimal point is used to separate whole numbers from decimals. Each decimal place is ten times smaller as you go one place to the right, just like whole numbers. So hundredths are ten times smaller than tenths, which are ten times smaller than ones.

tens	ones		tenths	hundredths
	8	.	3	2
1	4	.	0	5
2	3	.	7	

Did you know?

3.14159265358979323846264338327950288419716…

This famous decimal number is **Pi** (π), which is the ratio of the **circumference** to the **diameter** of a circle. It is not an exact number and for thousands of years mathematicians have tried to find the value of Pi to as many decimal places as possible. The current record holder for the most digits of Pi memorised is Akira Haraguchi who recited the number to 83,431 decimal places in July 2005. To recite all the known digits of Pi (6.4 billion digits) would take 133 years with no sleep.

Bargain Hunt

The sales were on and Isabella was on the hunt for a bargain. There were three pairs of trainers she liked, all at the same price. She needed to find out which pair were the cheapest in the sales.

Active Pumps £80 with 35% off

Sports Pumps £80 Price cut by £25

Power Pumps £80 reduced by 25%. Now a further 10% off

The Sports Pumps were easy to work out. "£80 subtract £25 is £55, not a bad price for these," thought Isabella.

She then looked at the Active Pumps. She only knew how to work out 10% by dividing by 10, so she asked Max for help to work out 35%.

"Knowing 10% is very helpful," he explained. "10% of £80 is £8 and 30% is just 3 times more than that, which is £24."

Isabella caught on quickly. "So 5% is half of £8, which is £4. So 35% of £80 is £4 added to £24, which is £28," she said excitedly. "Now £28 is a good price for trainers!"

I'm sure I heard Max say 'try and keep the trainers Spotless'!

"Not so fast," interrupted Max. "Remember, this is the **discount**. You must subtract this from £80, so the trainers are actually £52, which is still a good price."

Isabella noticed that the Power Pumps were discounted by 25% and then a further 10% so she thought that they would also cost £52, with the 35% discount.

Max was a little wiser than this. "This isn't what it seems. 25% of £80 is the same as $\frac{1}{4}$ of £80, which is £20. Subtract this from £80 to leave £60. 10% of £60 is £6. So the actual price of these in the sales is £54."

Isabella preferred the Active Pumps and they were £2 cheaper. "I didn't think buying trainers would keep my brain so active!"

Top Tips

Try to learn these equivalent decimals, fractions and percentages:

Decimals	0.1	0.2	0.3	0.4	0.5	0.6	0.7	0.8	0.9	0.25	0.75
Fractions	$\frac{1}{10}$	$\frac{1}{5}$	$\frac{3}{10}$	$\frac{2}{5}$	$\frac{1}{2}$	$\frac{3}{5}$	$\frac{7}{10}$	$\frac{4}{5}$	$\frac{9}{10}$	$\frac{1}{4}$	$\frac{3}{4}$
Percentages	10%	20%	30%	40%	50%	60%	70%	80%	90%	25%	75%

Did you know?

Test scores are often marked as percentages so that different tests can be compared. For example, putting these results in order is easier if you look at the percentages. To change scores to percentages, make them into hundredths and convert them to percentages.

7 out of 10	15 out of 20	30 out of 50	20 out of 25
$\frac{70}{100}$	$\frac{75}{100}$	$\frac{60}{100}$	$\frac{80}{100}$
70%	75%	60%	80%

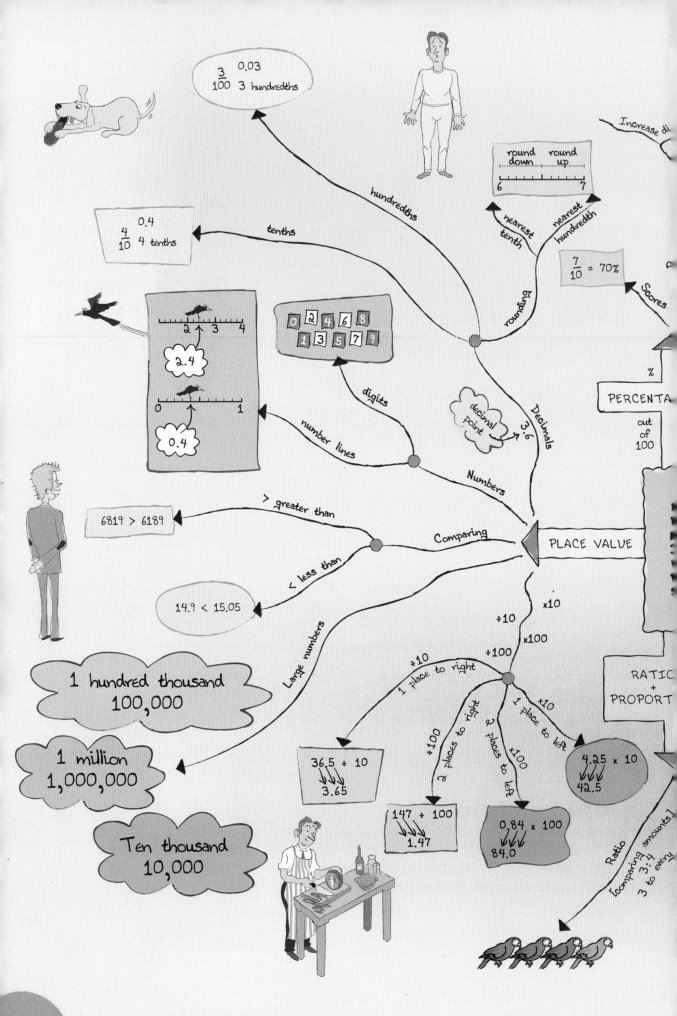

$\frac{3}{100}$ 0.03 3 hundredths

$\frac{4}{10}$ 0.4 4 tenths

round down   round up
6   7

hundredths

tenths

nearest tenth

nearest hundredth

rounding

$\frac{7}{10}$ = 70%

Scores

2.4

0.4

digits

decimal point
3.6

Decimals

%

PERCENTA

out of 100

number lines

Numbers

> greater than
6819 > 6189

< less than
14.9 < 15.05

Comparing

PLACE VALUE

Large numbers

1 hundred thousand
100,000

1 million
1,000,000

Ten thousand
10,000

×10
÷10
×100
÷100

÷10
1 place to right

÷100
2 places to right

×10
1 place to left

×100
2 places to left

36.5 ÷ 10
3.65

147 ÷ 100
1.47

0.84 × 100
84.0

4.25 × 10
42.5

RATIO
+ PROPORT

Ratio
[comparing amounts]
3:4
3 to every

Increase di

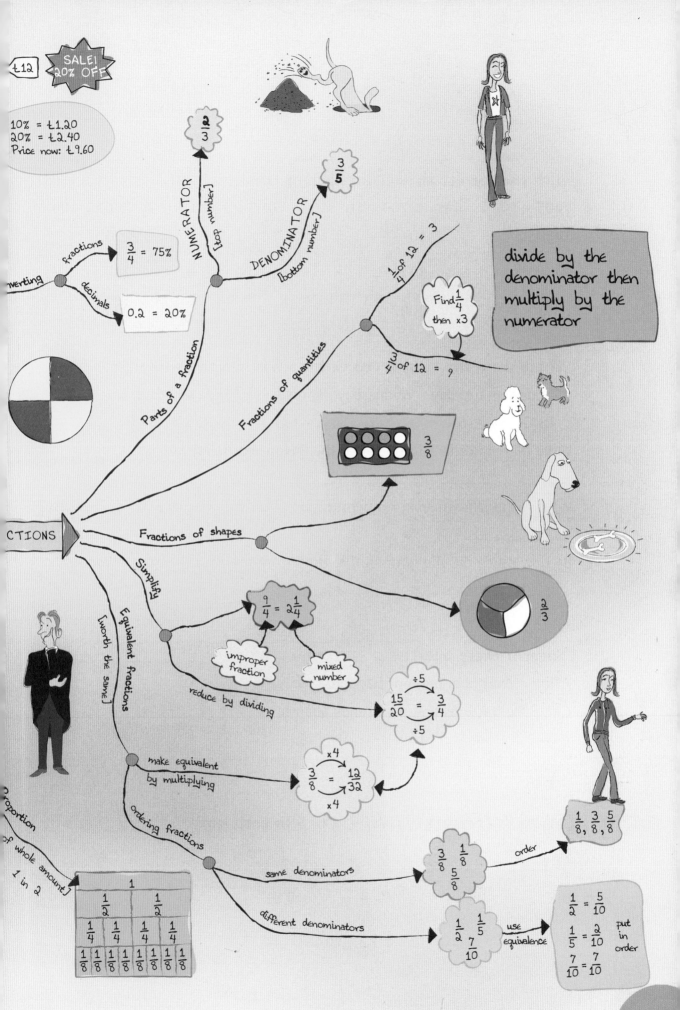

£12

SALE!
20% OFF

10% = £1.20
20% = £2.40
Price now: £9.60

NUMERATOR [top number]

$\frac{2}{3}$

DENOMINATOR [bottom number]

$\frac{3}{5}$

converting

fractions

decimals

$\frac{3}{4} = 75\%$

$0.2 = 20\%$

$\frac{1}{4}$ of 12 = 3

Find $\frac{1}{4}$ then ×3

$\frac{3}{4}$ of 12 = 9

divide by the denominator then multiply by the numerator

Parts of a fraction

Fractions of quantities

$\frac{3}{8}$

Fractions of shapes

$\frac{2}{3}$

CTIONS

Simplify

$\frac{9}{4} = 2\frac{1}{4}$

improper fraction

mixed number

Equivalent fractions [worth the same]

reduce by dividing

$\frac{15}{20} \xrightarrow{\div 5} = \frac{3}{4}$ ÷5

make equivalent by multiplying

$\frac{3}{8} \xrightarrow{\times 4} = \frac{12}{32}$ ×4

Proportion of whole amount] 1 in 2

ordering fractions

1							
$\frac{1}{2}$				$\frac{1}{2}$			
$\frac{1}{4}$		$\frac{1}{4}$		$\frac{1}{4}$		$\frac{1}{4}$	
$\frac{1}{8}$	$\frac{1}{8}$	$\frac{1}{8}$	$\frac{1}{8}$	$\frac{1}{8}$	$\frac{1}{8}$	$\frac{1}{8}$	$\frac{1}{8}$

same denominators

$\frac{3}{8}$ $\frac{1}{8}$ $\frac{5}{8}$

order

$\frac{1}{8}, \frac{3}{8}, \frac{5}{8}$

different denominators

$\frac{1}{2}$ $\frac{1}{5}$ $\frac{7}{10}$

use equivalence

$\frac{1}{2} = \frac{5}{10}$

$\frac{1}{5} = \frac{2}{10}$

$\frac{7}{10} = \frac{7}{10}$

put in order

Revise Time

1 Tick the correct answer for each of these.

a 7405 × 10
- 74005 ☐
- 74500 ☐
- 74050 ☐

b 30700 ÷ 10
- 307 ☐
- 3070 ☐
- 3007 ☐

c 14.3 × 100
- 1430 ☐
- 14300 ☐
- 14003 ☐

d 2961 ÷ 100
- 296.1 ☐
- 29 ☐
- 29.61 ☐

2 These were the temperatures for a week in the winter in Norway.

Monday	Tuesday	Wednesday	Thursday	Friday	Saturday	Sunday
−8°C	−5°C	0°C	−1°C	2°C	−6°C	−13°C

a Write them in order, starting with the lowest temperature.

_____ _____ _____ _____ _____ _____ _____

b What is the difference in temperature between the warmest and coldest day?

_____

c By how much did the temperature drop from the Saturday to the Sunday?

_____

3 Answer these questions.

a Join the pairs of equivalent fractions.

b Circle the fractions that are greater than $\frac{1}{2}$.

$\frac{15}{20}$ $\frac{6}{16}$ $\frac{3}{8}$

$\frac{20}{25}$ $\frac{3}{10}$ $\frac{30}{100}$

$\frac{1}{3}$ $\frac{3}{4}$ $\frac{3}{9}$ $\frac{4}{5}$

4 Write the correct symbol <, > or = in each box.

a $\frac{2}{5}$ ☐ $\frac{1}{4}$ ☐ $\frac{4}{16}$ ☐ $\frac{3}{10}$ ☐ $\frac{1}{2}$

b 0.2 ☐ 0.15 ☐ 0.08 ☐ 0.81 ☐ 0.9

c $\frac{1}{5}$ ☐ 0.2 ☐ $\frac{7}{10}$ ☐ 0.07 ☐ $\frac{3}{5}$

5 Complete this puzzle.

Across

2 $\frac{1}{4}$ of 420

4 $\frac{3}{5}$ of 70

5 $\frac{3}{4}$ of 24

6 $\frac{1}{10}$ of 4200

Down

1 $\frac{4}{5}$ of 100

2 $\frac{1}{2}$ of 248

3 $\frac{1}{3}$ of 1530

7 $\frac{2}{3}$ of 36

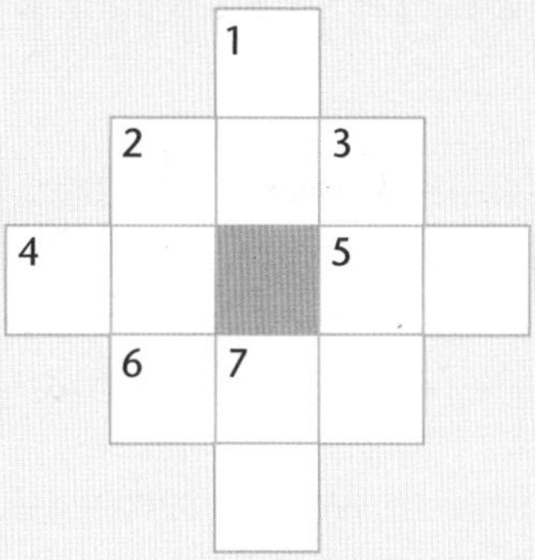

6 Answer these questions.

a What proportion of the flowers have:

6 petals   _____

4 petals   _____

12 petals   _____

b What are the ratios for these flower colours?

blue : red   _____

white : red   _____

blue : white _____

7 Write the decimal number shown for each arrow.

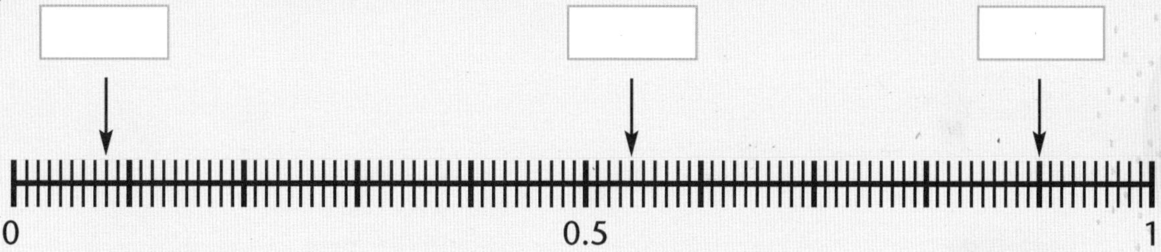

8 Complete this table.

fraction	percentage	decimal
_____	40%	_____
_____	_____	0.25
$\frac{4}{5}$	_____	_____

Sensational Sequences

Isabella ran into the laboratory excitedly. "I've just been reading about **Fibonacci numbers** in flowers. It's amazing!" she said to Sir Ralph. "The number of petals on lots of flowers are Fibonacci numbers – lilies have 3 petals, buttercups have 5 petals, marigolds have 13 petals, and as for daisies…"

"Wait, slow down," interrupted Sir Ralph. "Start at the beginning – what are Fibonacci numbers?"

Isabella then spent ten minutes explaining the number **sequence** discovered by Leonardo of Pisa at the beginning of the 13th century. "It's a simple sequence. Start at 0, then 1, and then add the last two numbers to get the next. So 1 + 1 = 2, 1 + 2 = 3, 2 + 3 = 5, and so on."

0, 1, 1, 2, 3, 5, 8, 13, 21, 34, 55, 89...

"You find these numbers in nature," she continued, "in petals, or the spirals of the seeds in sunflowers and pine cones, or the arrangement of leaves on plants."

Sir Ralph found this very interesting. "Perhaps you can spot the next number in this sequence. I'm growing bacteria and have recorded their growth every hour."

Hour	1	2	3	4	5	6
Length (mm)	2	4	8	16	32	

Isabella spotted the pattern immediately. "The numbers are doubling, so they are now 64mm long. In an hour they will be 128mm. That is almost 13cm, which is bigger than the dish!"

This rule is 'add 4'. I've jumped 6 times, so that's 24 muddy paw prints!

44

Max had been listening with interest. He told Isabella that reverse sequences were his favourite. "What do you think are the next few numbers in this sequence?"

22	17	12	7	—	—

Isabella saw that the rule was 'subtract 5'. "The next number is 2 and then you can't go any further."

Max disagreed. "Don't forget negative numbers. Count back past zero to –3 and then –8. It can go on forever… a bit like you and your Fibonacci numbers!"

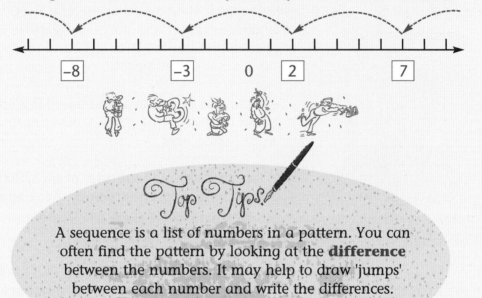

-8 -3 0 2 7

Top Tips!

A sequence is a list of numbers in a pattern. You can often find the pattern by looking at the **difference** between the numbers. It may help to draw 'jumps' between each number and write the differences.

39   32   25   18

Did you know?

Some number patterns are made from sequences of shapes.

Square numbers:

1   4   9   16

Notice that the differences are **consecutive** odd numbers.

$1 + 3 + 5 + 7$

Triangular numbers:

1   3   6   10

Notice that the differences increase by one each time.

$1 + 2 + 3 + 4$

Follow the Rules

Isabella was playing with numbers on the whiteboard in the laboratory. She wrote the numbers 0 to 9 down the board and then next to them the numbers 9 to 0.

```
09

18

27
```

She stood back and gasped. "Wow! I've accidentally written out the 9 times table."

Sir Ralph was watching and explained that the **multiples** of 9 were his favourite multiples. "Have you noticed that the **digits** of numbers divisible by 9 always add up to 9? It's a great way of checking if a number is **divisible** by 9. For example, 2655 – the digits add up to 18, and 1 + 8 is 9… magic!"

Isabella was impressed, and asked if you could check for multiples of other numbers in the same way.

"You are talking about rules of divisibility," Sir Ralph replied, mysteriously. "You already know the rules for numbers that are multiples of 2, 5 and 10."

Isabella thought for a moment. "Of course, multiples of 2 are always even, multiples of 5 always end in 0 or 5 and multiples of 10 always end in 0."

"Exactly," replied Sir Ralph. "Multiples of 3 are also easy to spot. If you add up the digits, the total can always be divided by 3. Make it a single digit and it is always 3, 6 or 9. For example, 897 – the digits add up to 24, and 2 + 4 is 6."

Isabella knew that the 6 times table was double the 3 times table and they were all even numbers. She realised that multiples of 6 must have the same rule as multiples of 3, but only if the number is even. For example, 342 is even and the digits add up to 9.

"The rule for multiples of 4," Sir Ralph continued, "is that the last two digits can always be divided by 4, such as 38516. The rule for multiples of 8 is similar but only useful for huge numbers – if the last three digits of the number can be divided by 8, then it is a multiple of 8. This leaves us only the rule for multiples of 7... which is far too complicated for you to worry about."

Sir Ralph hoped that Isabella wouldn't push him about the rule for multiples of 7... because he didn't have a clue!

Top Tips

Multiples are numbers made by multiplying together two other numbers. So, examples of multiples of 3 are 30 (made by multiplying 3 and 10), 48 (multiplying 3 and 16) and 99 (multiplying 3 and 33).

Did you know?

For those of you that want to know the rule of divisibility for multiples of 7, here is one method:

Take the last digit, double it, and subtract it from the rest of the number. If the answer is divisible by 7 (including 0), then the number is a multiple of 7.

378 ➜ double 8 is 16

37 − 16 = 21

21 is divisible by 7, so 378 is a multiple of 7.

Leaning Ladders

It was a strange sight, seeing Max's face outside the laboratory window peering in, particularly as it was on the second floor. Sir Ralph explained to Isabella that Max had bought a new extendable ladder and was cleaning the windows. He then pointed out some information he'd written on the whiteboard.

a = length of ladder d = distance between wall and base of ladder $d = \frac{a}{4}$

	Laboratory	Bedrooms	Office
Length of ladder	480cm	600cm	360cm
Distance between wall and ladder	120cm		

Ladder length → in → ÷4 → out → Distance from wall

"In the safety notes, $d = \frac{a}{4}$ was the **formula** given for working out the distance the ladder should be away from the wall," explained Sir Ralph. "Max doesn't enjoy algebra much, but I love it, so I drew out a **function** machine and table of results to help him. The distance between the base of the ladder and the wall is $\frac{a}{4}$ or $a \div 4$. Max measured the length of the ladder for each window and now we can work out where to stand the ladder."

"I've finished here," shouted Max through the window. "Where do I need to put the ladder for the bedrooms?"

Isabella looked at the formula and the table of results and divided 600 by 4. "150cm away from the wall," she replied. She then worked where the ladder should be for the office: 360cm ÷ 4, which is 90cm.

Is there a formu[la]
for the length of [a]
I can hang her[e]
without a ladde[r]

Sir Ralph was busy writing up another formula.

$$4b = 12$$

"What does that mean?" Isabella asked.

"It's the number of buckets of water Max has used," explained Sir Ralph. "He has used 4 buckets for 12 windows. Each bucketful cleans 3 windows, so b = 3."

All of a sudden, Isabella leapt up and shouted, "Aha... I've got it! I've been trying to solve the **equation** 3x + 2 = 17 for my homework and all this formula work has helped me. To find x, subtract 2 from both sides and then divide by 3, which means... x = 5!"

Sir Ralph smiled, thinking to himself, "She'll make a fine professor some day!"

Top Tips

Follow these three steps to work out equations:
2y − 3 = 5
1 Get letters on one side, numbers on the other.
Add 3 to both sides: 2y = 8
2 Say the equation as a sentence. 2 times something makes 8. 2 fours make 8.
3 Write the value of the letter and check it in the equation.
y = 4   (2 × 4) − 3 = 5

Did you know?

The word 'equation' comes from a Latin word meaning 'to set equal'. Equations always have an equal sign (=), and both sides of the equation must be balanced or equal. If you add or subtract a number from one side, do the same to the other and the equation stays balanced. It's a good way of working out the value of a letter in an equation.

Bingo!

19	25		29
	9	48	75
24	30	12	
3		10	21

BINGO!

It was raining heavily and Isabella wanted to play a game. "I'm bored with my board games, Dad. Got any other ideas?" she asked.

Sir Ralph was struggling with his **formula** for the average speed of a raindrop down a windowpane, so he was pleased to help. "What about Special Number Bingo?" There was no time to reply as Sir Ralph's head disappeared into a cupboard. He emerged with a lovely old bingo box and excitedly explained the rules.

"Write any number from 1 to 100 in the blank spaces and I'll shuffle these clue cards."

Square number	Prime number	Multiple of 3	Factor of 24	Triangular number
Odd number	Even number	Multiple of 4	Factor of 60	Multiple of 5

They turned over the top card, '**Multiple** of 3'.

"Cross out any number that can be divided exactly by 3," explained Sir Ralph. Isabella chose 21 and turned over the next card, '**Factor** of 24'.

Isabella looked puzzled, so Sir Ralph helped her out. "A factor of 24 is any number that will divide exactly into 24, so it could be 1, 2, 3, 4, 6, 8, 12 or 24. Write them as pairs of factors to see them all: (1, 24) (2, 12) (3, 8) (4, 6)."

Sir Ralph decided to explain the other tricky clue cards. "Numbers multiplied by themselves make **square numbers**, such as 1 (1×1), 4 (2×2), 9 (3×3), 16 (4×4) and so on. **Prime numbers** are any numbers that can only be divided exactly by themselves or 1, such as 11, 19 and 23. **Triangular numbers** are made by triangular patterns, such as 1, 3, 6, 10 and 15."

They called for Max so they could all
play, but soon wished they hadn't!
He won every game because he
chose numbers that could
match more than one clue. 15
was one of his favourites – an
odd number, multiple of
both 3 and 5, factor of 60
and a triangular number.

Top Tips

Every whole number has an even number of factors,
unless it is a square number.
18 → (1, 18) (2, 9) (3, 6)
16 → (1, 16) (2, 8) (4)
Prime numbers always have a single pair of factors –
1 and itself.

Did you know?

Square numbers and triangular numbers are related sets of number patterns.
Square numbers

$1 \times 1 = 1 \quad 2 \times 2 = 4 \quad 3 \times 3 = 9 \quad 4 \times 4 = 16 \quad 5 \times 5 = 25$

Triangular numbers

$1 + 2 = 3 \quad 1 + 2 + 3 = 6 \quad 1 + 2 + 3 + 4 = 10 \quad 1 + 2 + 3 + 4 + 5 = 15$

If you add consecutive pairs of triangular numbers they make a square
number. For example, $10 + 15 = 25$

Spin a Winner

Isabella's Pony Club were organising a Fun Day to raise money for new equipment.

Max was running the tombola and Isabella had made a spin-for-a-sweet game. She had a board divided into 12 parts and a spinning arrow.

Isabella was trying to come up with the rules. "What about spin on red to win a sweet?" she asked Max.

Max explained that this gave an even or 50:50 chance of winning. "6 out of 12 is the same as $\frac{1}{2}$ or a 1 in 2 chance. There is an equal **likelihood** of winning and losing."

Isabella wasn't happy with this, as too many people would win prizes. She found some blue paint and painted two of the red and two of the yellow sections blue.

"This is better," she thought. "Spin on blue to win gives a 4 in 12 chance of winning. That's the same as $\frac{1}{3}$ or a 1 in 3 chance. This means that it is likely that 2 out of every 3 people won't win, so at least I won't run out of prizes."

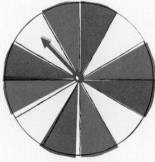

Max had two sets of raffle tickets numbered 1 to 200. He put one whole set of tickets into a bucket. Then, from the other set, he took out all the tickets ending in 0 or 5 to stick onto the 40 prizes. If anyone picked out a number ending in 0 or 5, they won the matching prize.

There's probably more chance of Spotless knocking off a coconut than me hitting one!

COCONUT SHY
3 BALLS
50P

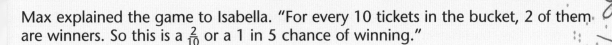

Max explained the game to Isabella. "For every 10 tickets in the bucket, 2 of them are winners. So this is a $\frac{2}{10}$ or a 1 in 5 chance of winning."

"So there is a better chance of winning on my game than your tombola," she noted. "I think more people will want to play my game."

"Don't you be so sure, Izzy," replied Max smugly. "I've got some pretty good prizes."

Top Tips

If two dice are rolled and the numbers totalled, the numbers 1 to 12 can be made in 36 different ways.

Dice	1	2	3	4	5	6
1	2	3	4	5	6	7
2	3	4	5	6	7	8
3	4	5	6	7	8	9
4	5	6	7	8	9	10
5	6	7	8	9	10	11
6	7	8	9	10	11	12

For example, 5 can be made in four ways, and 4 can be made in three ways. This means there is more chance of totalling 5 (a 1 in 9 chance) than 4 (a 1 in 12 chance). There is only a 1 in 36 chance of totalling 12, and it is impossible to roll a total of 1. Try this yourself with two dice.

Did you know?

A probability scale shows how likely it is that an event will happen. Remember: 0 is impossible – there is no chance of it happening, and 1 is certain – it will definitely happen. An even chance is when there is an equal chance of something happening or not happening. We also say a 1 in 2 chance or a 50:50 chance.

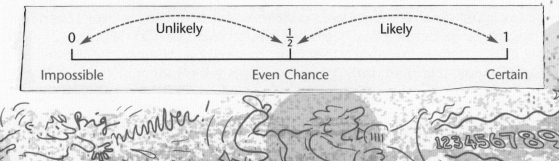

Cycle Safety

Sir Ralph had almost finished his latest invention – a cycle safety jacket. It was reflective, had flashing indicator lights and inflated on impact if you fell.

Isabella tried the jacket on, but it was tiny and uncomfortable. "It's a bit like wearing a life jacket on your bike I don't think it will catch on," she laughed.

"Hmmm... I'd better sort out the sizes next," thought Sir Ralph.

He asked Isabella to collect some data from her school. He wanted the height of five children from each year so that he had a good range of sizes.

Isabella carried out the survey and brought home a frequency chart showing the results.

Children's Heights

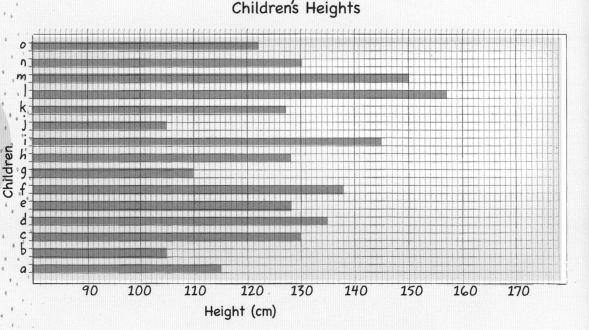

Height (cm)

Sir Ralph looked at the graph, but found that it didn't help him very much. "I can't make all these different sizes. I was hoping to make just three sizes: small, medium and large."

Max coughed quietly. "If I may make a suggestion. Try putting all the heights into three groups. Then you can have a range of heights for small, medium and large."

Sir Ralph clapped his hands. "Brilliant... could you show me how you do that?"

Max could see that there were no children under 100cm or over 160cm in height, so he decided that the three groups could be 100–120cm, 121–140cm and 141–160cm. He used a tally chart to show the number of children within each range, and then drew a graph to show the results.

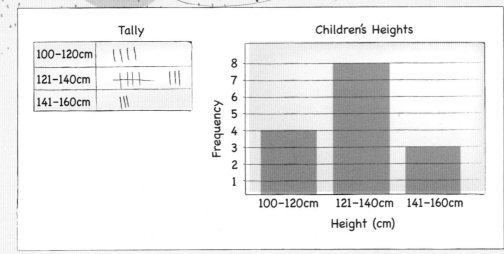

Tally	
100–120cm	||||
121–140cm	⧫⧫⧫⧫ |||
141–160cm	|||

Children's Heights

Frequency (vertical axis: 1–8)

Height (cm): 100–120cm, 121–140cm, 141–160cm

Dad... help!

Sir Ralph was delighted. "This makes it much easier to work out what I need to make. Medium is the most common size, so I'll make twice as many medium jackets as small or large jackets."

Isabella smiled as she tried to imagine her friends wearing these fluorescent life jackets!

Top Tips

To understand bar charts, remember:
1 Read the title. What is it all about?
2 Look at the axis labels. What are the horizontal and vertical lines showing?
3 Work out the scale. Do the numbers go up in 1s, 2s, 5s, 10s...?
4 Compare the bars. What amounts do they show?

Did you know?

Pie charts are circles divided into sections. Each section shows a number of items, which could be shown as a fraction, percentage or an amount. Always look at the total for the whole 'pie' and then work out the fraction of each section to find the amount.

Travelling to school

30% car
50% walk
20% bike

Trail Trial

Isabella was now 11 years old and it was a Witherbottom tradition that all 11-year-olds in the family complete the 'Trail Trial'. Sir Ralph showed Isabella his own time/distance graph from when he was 11, and also Max's graph, whose father was the butler when Max was 11 years old.

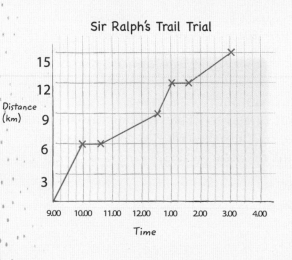

Sir Ralph's Trail Trial

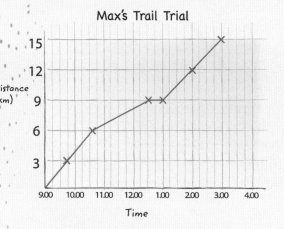

Max's Trail Trial

"We both finished the 15km course in exactly the same time: 6 hours. My grandfather has the quickest time. He finished at 2.00pm." Sir Ralph continued. "You only pass the trial if you finish before 4.00pm."

They looked at the graphs. Sir Ralph had decided to run the first part, so completed 6km by 10.00am. He then rested before the very steep hill through the woods between 6km and 9km. Max explained that he took it steadily, walking all the way and resting only once for lunch after the hill climb. It was then downhill and a little quicker, although Sir Ralph needed a second rest before the final 3km.

Isabella studied the graphs and decided that the only way to save time and complete the course was to walk steadily like Max, but not stop for such a long rest.

Before the trial, she trained by running and walking with Spotless. He was getting fit as well! On the day of the trial there were time markers at 3km, 6km, 9km and 12km to record her times and Sir Ralph and Max were at the finish to greet her. Isabella completed the course very well and looked tired but jubilant at the finish.

"Well done!" shouted Sir Ralph. "You've beaten our times by a clear 15 minutes."

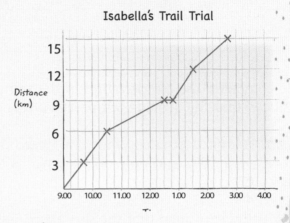

Isabella's Trail Trial

Top Tips!

A graph with numbers on both axes is often shown as a line graph. Follow these three steps to read line graphs accurately:
1 Read all the information provided so you understand what the graph is about.
2 Use a ruler to go up from the horizontal axis to meet the line.
3 From this point read across to the vertical axis to give the value.

Did you know?

Conversion graphs show one amount converted to another. They are straight line graphs and are easy to draw, once you get the scales for the axes right. For converting pints into litres, 2 litres is approximately 3.5 pints. Mark a cross at this point and then draw a line from zero through the cross. Different values can then be converted.

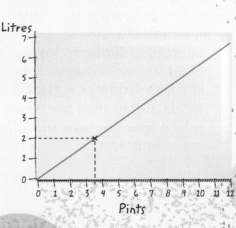

Whatever the Weather

Sir Ralph had recorded the temperature every day for two weeks in February:

Mo	Tu	We	Th	Fr	Sa	Su	Mo	Tu	We	Th	Fr	Sa	Su
10°C	10°C	8°C	3°C	3°C	5°C	6°C	7°C	9°C	10°C	10°C	12°C	10°C	9°C

He compared the temperatures of the same two weeks in the previous year and noticed that the average temperature was exactly the same: 8°C.

Isabella looked puzzled when she heard this. "That can't be right, Dad. More days were 10°C and only one day was 8°C, so surely the average temperature is 10°C."

Sir Ralph explained that she was absolutely right if you used the **mode** as the average. "The mode is the most frequent or common result. Five days were at 10°C, so this is the mode temperature. I actually used the **mean average**. I added all the temperatures together, which came to 112° and then divided by 14, which is the number of days. 112 ÷ 14 = 8, so the mean average temperature is 8°C. If all the temperatures were spread evenly over all 14 days, each day would be 8°C."

"How do you know which one to use?" asked Isabella.

Sir Ralph thought for a moment. "It depends on which would give you the most useful information. The mean average is mathematically accurate, but the mode is useful for things like the average number of days of rain in a month or average shoe size in a class. If a shoe shop wants to order some more shoes it may look at which size is the most popular, the mode, rather than the mean, which may not be a whole number or size."

This says an average portion is 45g. That sounds 'mean' to me!

Sir Ralph then explained a third way of showing an average: the middle or **median**. "The important thing with using the median is to start by putting all the numbers in order from smallest to largest. This is called the **range**."

3°C 3°C 5°C 6°C 7°C 8°C 9°C 9°C 10°C 10°C 10°C 10°C 10°C 12°C

"If there is an odd amount, the median is the middle number. If there is an even amount, like this, take the middle two and work out their mean, which is 9°C."

Isabella laughed. "So the average could be 8°C, 9°C or 10°C, depending on the method you use. I love maths!"

Top Tips

Sometimes the mean, mode and median can give the same results. For example, these are the scores for five maths tests, marked out of 20:

14   15   16   16   19

Mean: 14 + 15 + 16 + 16 + 19 = 80 ÷ 5 = 16
Mode: 16 occurs twice
Median: 16 is the middle score

Did you know?

The mean is sometimes called the arithmetic mean and is used to study data from a survey, graph or table. It can give a false average if a number is much lower or higher than all the others, and often the mean isn't a whole number. A strange example is 2.4 as the average number of children in a family in the UK. Not many families have 0.4 children!

add 5 to both sides →
$$2x - 5 = 7$$
$$2x = 12$$
$$x = 6$$

IN OUT
$6 \rightarrow$ +4 $\rightarrow 10$
function

A formula is a rule using letters
e.g. Area of rect = length x wi
$A = lw$

letters on one side, numbers on the other

Balanced equations

Function machines

Form

1, 1, 2, 3, 5, 8, 13

$1 + 2 = 3$ $1 + 2 + 3 = 6$ $1 + 2 + 3 + 4 = 10$ $1 + 2 + 3 + 4 + 5 = 15$

square numbers

triangular numbers

shapes

Fibonacci

counting

look at differences

| 1 | 5 | 9 | 13 | ? |
4   4   4   4

| -11 | -6 | -1 | 4 | ? |
5   5   5   5

FORMUL + EQUATIO

1
1x1   2x2   3x3   4x4
4   9   16

Factors
15   32
(1, 15) (1, 32)
(3, 5)   (2, 16)
         (4, 8)

square numbers

$4 \times 4 = 16$
$4^2 = 16$

Sequences

Numbers that divide exactly into other numbers

factors

Special numbers

NUMBER PATTERNS

P
A
T
T
E
R
N
S

•

D
A
T
A

even   odd

ending in 0, 2, 4, 6, 8

ending in 1, 3, 5, 7, 9

Multiples

A whole number is divisible by:
• 2 if the last digit is even
• 3 if the sum of its digits can be divided by 3
• 4 if the last 2 digits can be divided by 4
• 5 if the last digit is 0 or 5
• 6 if it is even and divisible by 3
• 8 if half of it is divisible by 4
• 9 if the sum of its digits is divisible by 9
• 10 if the last digit is 0

PROBABIL

multiplying

rules of divisibility

Multiples of:
4: 4, 8, 12, 16, 20 .....
5: 5, 10, 15, 20 25

1 in 3 chance of rolling a multiple of 3

Dice experiment

They go on and on past the tables

1 in 6 chance of rolling a 3

1 in 2 chance of rolling even numbers

Probability scale

20 is the lowest common multiple of 4 and 5

0        $\frac{1}{2}$ 1
Impossible   Even   Certain

• 1 in 2 cha
• 50:50
• equal chance of somethin happening a not happenin

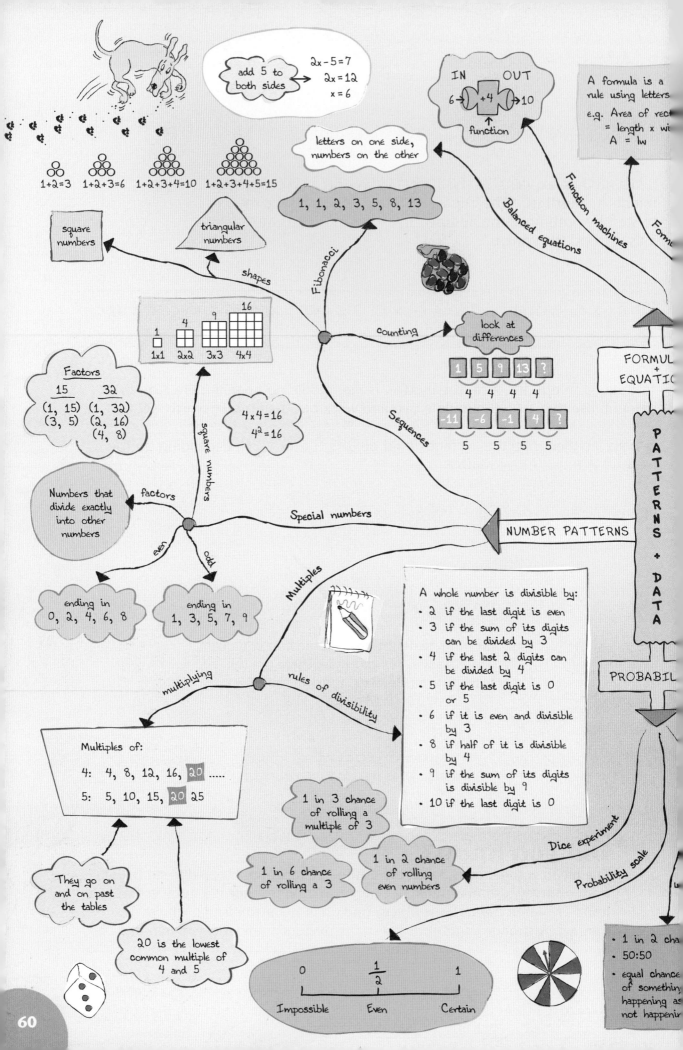

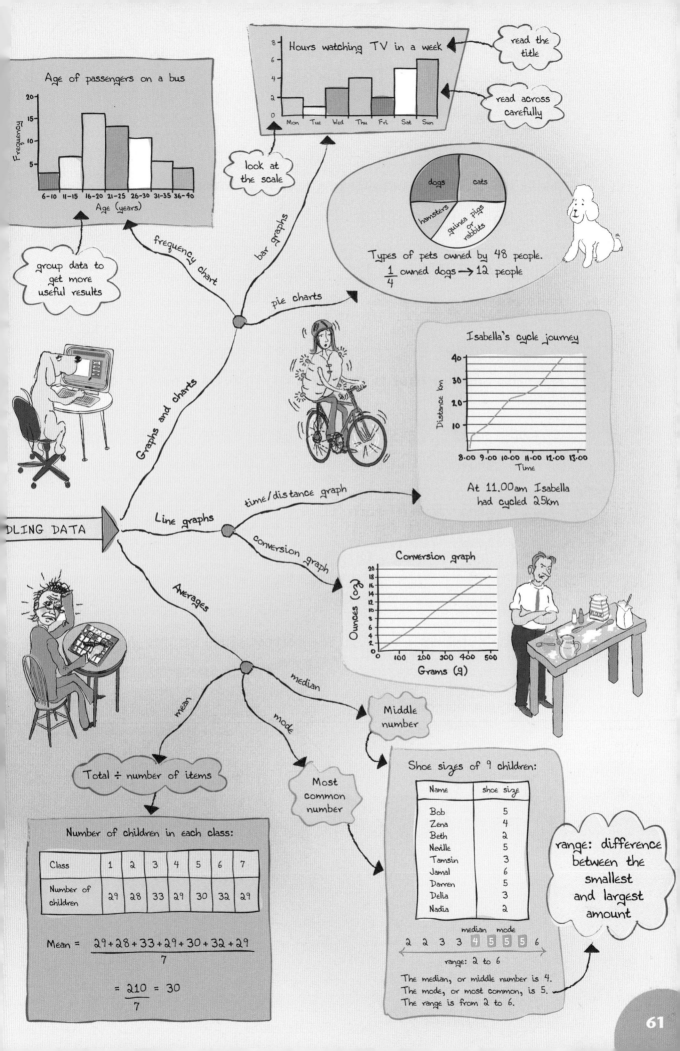

Age of passengers on a bus

Hours watching TV in a week

read the title

read across carefully

look at the scale

Types of pets owned by 48 people.
$\frac{1}{4}$ owned dogs → 12 people

dogs   cats   hamsters   guinea pigs or rabbits

frequency chart

bar graphs

pie charts

group data to get more useful results

Isabella's cycle journey

At 11.00am Isabella had cycled 25km

Graphs and charts

time/distance graph

Line graphs

conversion graph

Conversion graph

HANDLING DATA

Averages

mean

mode

median

Middle number

Total ÷ number of items

Most common number

Shoe sizes of 9 children:

Name	shoe size
Bob	5
Zena	4
Beth	2
Neville	5
Tamsin	3
Jamal	6
Darren	5
Delia	3
Nadia	2

median   mode
2 2 3 3 4 5 5 5 6
range: 2 to 6

The median, or middle number is 4.
The mode, or most common, is 5.
The range is from 2 to 6.

range: difference between the smallest and largest amount

Number of children in each class:

Class	1	2	3	4	5	6	7
Number of children	29	28	33	29	30	32	29

Mean = $\dfrac{29+28+33+29+30+32+29}{7}$

$= \dfrac{210}{7} = 30$

Revise Time

1 Write the missing numbers in these sequences.

a 23   18   _13_   8   _3_   _-2_   -7   _-12_

b 8   ___   26   35   ___   53   ___   ___

c ___   4   ___   16   25   36   ___   ___

2 Ring the number that is neither a multiple of 3 nor a multiple of 4.

124   372   215   608   441   816   243   392

3 Work out the value of each letter.

a $3n = 15$ b $7 + y = 18$ c $\frac{a}{3} = 9$ d $4x + 2 = 14$

n = 5   y = 11   a = 27   x = 3

4 Write the numbers 1 to 25 in the correct place on this Venn diagram.

square numbers   multiples of 3

factors of 36

62

5 Look at this bag of beads.

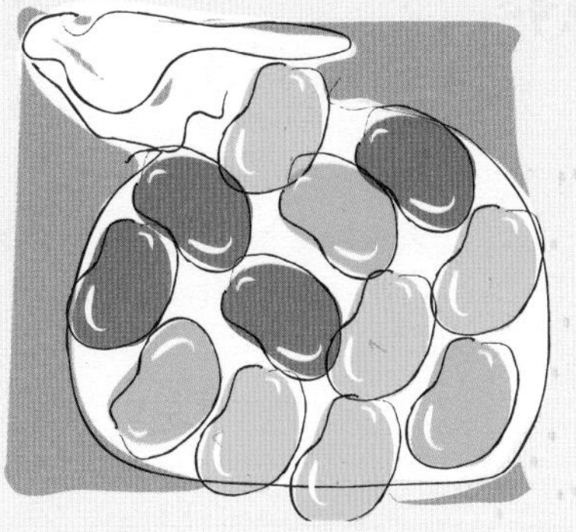

a What is the probability of picking a red bead? _____

b What is the probability of picking a green bead? _____

c Two red beads are taken out. What is the probability of picking a yellow bead? _____

6 This graph shows the monthly sales of ice-creams from a van. In which month were the following number of ice-creams sold?

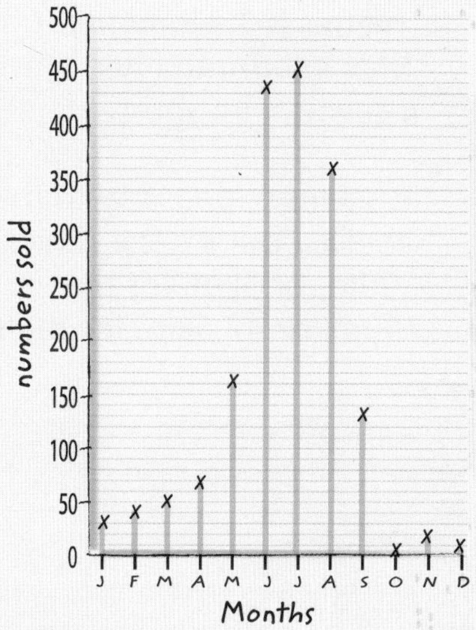

a 436 _____   d 50 _____

b 360 _____   e 68 _____

c 162 _____   f 131 _____

7 In which month was there the biggest increase in sales?

_____

8 This chart shows the temperature in Portugal for a week in February.

Mon	Tues	Weds	Thurs	Fri	Sat	Sun
13°C	17°C	18°C	17°C	17°C	16°C	14°C

For the temperature, work out the following:

a Mode   _____

b Mean average _____

c Median   _____

Running Routes

Max had been out running with a pedometer to measure the distance of three different routes.

"That's the last one done," he panted. He looked as if he'd just completed a marathon. "Could you write these distances on my map in kilometres, please Izzy? I don't think I have the strength."

Isabella was happy to help. "1500 metres is 1 kilometre 500 metres, so..." Max interrupted her. "Just write 1.5 km, it seems a lot shorter!"

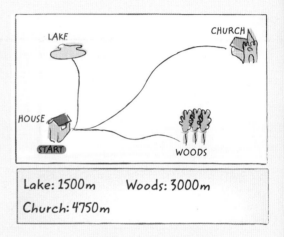

Lake: 1500m   Woods: 3000m
Church: 4750m

"It seems a long way to me," laughed Isabella, "but it's the shortest route. 3000m, or 3km, for the woods path and 4750m, or 47.5km, for the church path."

Luckily Max's breathing had settled down enough for him to hear Isabella's error. "Hopefully you mean 4.75km. 47.5km is the distance to town and back four times, which is tiring in a car, let alone on foot!"

Isabella got them both a healthy yoghurt drink from the fridge. Isabella noticed that her yoghurt pot was measured in grams, with 80g on the label, but the other used millilitres, with a capacity of 75ml. Max agreed that this was strange, as liquids were usually measured in litres and millilitres.

"Perhaps yours is a bit thicker. It isn't a liquid so the mass is measured rather than the capacity," he added. "80 grams is only 0.08kg, which is less than a tenth of a kilogram. A gram is such a tiny amount."

Sir Ralph walked into the room. "Give me good old-fashioned imperial measures any day – inches, feet, yards, miles, pints, gallons, ounces, pounds and stones – everyone understood them," blustered Sir Ralph.

Max smiled. "The metric system is simple. To convert from, say, grams to kilograms or litres to millilitres you just multiply and divide amounts by 10, 100 or 1000. I remember you getting in a complete muddle with the number of ounces in a pound, or yards in a mile."

Sir Ralph reluctantly agreed. He had forgotten how difficult it had been. "It's strange though that we still use pints for our milk and miles for long distances," he added.

Top Tips

Milli means one thousandth
Centi means one hundredth
Kilo means one thousand
Use this to help you learn these equivalent measures:

Length
1 centimetre (cm) = 10 millimetres (mm)
1 metre (m) = 100cm
1 kilometre (km) = 1000m

Mass
1 kilogram (kg) = 1000 grams (g)
1 tonne = 1000kg

Capacity
1 litre (l) = 1000 millilitres (ml)
1 centilitre (cl) = 100ml

Did you know?

Some imperial units are still used, so try to learn these approximate equivalent measures:

Length	Mass	Capacity
12 inches = 1 foot	16 ounces = 1 pound (lb)	8 pints = 1 gallon
2.5cm ≈ 1 inch	28g ≈ 1 ounce	1.75 pints ≈ 1 litre
30cm ≈ 1 foot	2.25 lb ≈ 1kg	4.5 litres ≈ 1 gallon
3 feet ≈ 1 metre		

(≈ means "is approximately equal to")

Sound the Alarm!

Isabella yawned as her programme finished on TV. It was half past eight and she felt ready for bed, so she shouted goodnight to anyone who could hear her and trudged up the stairs. She had reached the top step when Max called her. "I've bought you a new alarm clock – your old one never worked properly."

A few minutes later Isabella came down to show Max the alarm clock. "This one's broken as well," she complained. "It says 20:30."

Max smiled. "It's not broken, it's just a 24-hour clock. After 12 o'clock midday, the hours carry on to 13:00, rather than 1.00pm, then 14:00, rather than 2.00pm, then 15:00, 16:00 and so on. So 20:30 is actually 8.30pm."

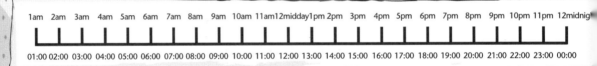

1am 2am 3am 4am 5am 6am 7am 8am 9am 10am 11am 12midday 1pm 2pm 3pm 4pm 5pm 6pm 7pm 8pm 9pm 10pm 11pm 12midnight

01:00 02:00 03:00 04:00 05:00 06:00 07:00 08:00 09:00 10:00 11:00 12:00 13:00 14:00 15:00 16:00 17:00 18:00 19:00 20:00 21:00 22:00 23:00 00:00

"Why do we need 24-hour time?" asked Isabella.

Max thought for a moment. "I suppose it stops any confusion. For example, If you booked a train for 7.15, you wouldn't know if it was morning or evening. That's why 'am' and 'pm' are used for 12-hour time. With 24-hour time there's no confusion because the morning time is 07:15 and the evening time is 19:15."

Isabella sat in bed and read until the clock showed 21:15. "That seems a lot later than 9.15pm," she thought. She then set the alarm for 07:30 and quickly fell asleep.

> I don't believe Sir Ralph can tell the time. He's always late!

In the morning Isabella got up when the alarm sounded at 07:30. She shouted downstairs to Max, "I'll have breakfast at zero seven fifty please."

"She's a quick learner," thought Max, smiling to himself.

Isabella spent the whole of breakfast using 24-hour time whenever she could. She sounded like an airline pilot or a train guard!

As Max dropped her off at school, he couldn't help using 24-hour time himself. "Have a good day. I'll pick you up at precisely fifteen thirty."

"That sounded rather good," he thought. "Perhaps I should have been a pilot!"

Top Tips

'am' stands for ante meridian and means morning – from 12 midnight to 12 noon.
'pm' stands for post meridian and means afternoon – from 12 noon to 12 midnight.
Instead of using am and pm, 24-hour time goes from 0000 to 2400. When reading 24-hour time, remember 'am' times look the same, but you add 12 hours to the 'pm' times. Also, you always use 4 numbers when you write the 24-hour clock, even for morning times.

Did you know?

Use a 'knuckle method' to learn the number of days in the months:
31 days: January, March, May, July, August, October, December
All the 'knuckle months' have 31 days.
February has 28 days (29 days in a leap year) and April, June, September and November have 30 days.

The Lawn Raider

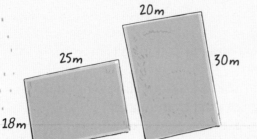

Sir Ralph looked out at his lawns and noticed some bare patches on the grass. "Time to give it some tender loving care," he thought. "I'll buy some lawn feed."

He decided to measure the **area** of the lawns in square metres so he could buy the correct amount of fertiliser.

Isabella helped by holding one end of the tape measure. Spotless was absolutely no help by running off with the other end. Eventually they managed to write down the lengths of each side. "The sides of this lawn are 25 metres and 18 metres," noted Sir Ralph. "It's a rectangle, so the area is 25 × 18."

He scribbled down a calculation and worked out that the area of this lawn was 450m². Isabella wanted to work out the area of the next lawn. "The two sides are 30m and 20m, so I need to multiply them together. I know that 3 × 2 is 6, so 30 × 20 is 600m²."

The final lawn was a bit trickier to work out.

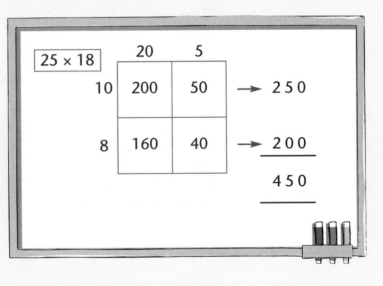

"This is an odd shape," said Sir Ralph, "so we need to break it up into rectangles. I can see two rectangles, 8m × 10m and 12m × 4m. So the total area is 80m² added to 48m², which is 128m²."

They'll be so pleased when I've chased this mole away.

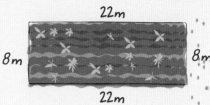

22m

8m 8m

22m

There was just one more job before going to the garden centre: measuring the **perimeter** – the distance all the way round the edge of the vegetable patch. "I need a fence to keep those pesky rabbits off – they just ignore Spotless," muttered Sir Ralph.

"To find the perimeter you just need to add up the lengths of each side," he explained to Isabella. They measured each side and quickly worked out the perimeter: 60 metres.

Suddenly a cheeky mole popped up in the middle of the lawn. Sir Ralph groaned. "Forget feeding the lawn," he said. "I'm going back to the lab to invent a 'mole-deterring device'."

Top Tips

If you need to work out the area of a shape that has curved sides, count all the squares that are bigger than a half.
The area of this shape is approximately 15 squares.

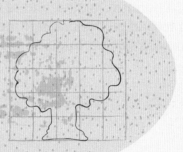

Did you know?

Use these **formulae** to find the perimeter or area of a rectangle or square:
Perimeter = 2(l + w)
Add the length and width together and then double it.
Area = l × w
Multiply the length and the width together.

w

l

All Boxed Up

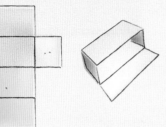

Max was having a spring clean in Sir Ralph's laboratory. He had bought a variety of flat-pack boxes so that everything could be sorted and tidied away neatly. Isabella wanted to help, so she made up the folded cardboard boxes. The instructions said 'fold on each dotted line', so she started on the first box.

"That's just what I need, a cuboid for these rock samples," Max said to Isabella. "Now, these microscope parts would fit nicely into a cube box if you've got one of those."

Isabella thought she had seen a **net** of a cube. "6 square **faces**, all the same size. Which one of these is the right one?"

"If you fold them up, I think you'll find that they're both cubes. There are several different ways of making nets of cubes," Max said knowledgeably.

He was absolutely right, and Isabella spent the next 20 minutes folding and re-folding cubes, trying to find all the different nets. This wasn't particularly helpful for Max, but Isabella was having fun! She found 9 more different ways of making a cube net.

Max laughed. "I'm glad you didn't try to investigate all the nets of a regular **dodecahedron**. There are 43,380 different nets!"

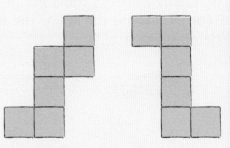

Isabella found a different net that puzzled her. "Do you think this is a pyramid?" she asked Max.

They made the shape by folding up the five faces. "This is a triangular prism," said Max. "Do you notice that it has three rectangle faces and two triangle faces? You can recognise a prism because the two end faces are the same size and shape, with rectangles joining the two end faces."

Isabella wasn't really listening. She was already planning how to use it as an indoor kennel for Spotless!

Did they say prism or prison?

Top Tips

Solid shapes are 3-dimensional, and include cones, spheres and cylinders. A polyhedron is a solid shape with sides made from **polygons** – flat shapes with straight **edges**.

tetrahedron   cube   cuboid   triangular prism   square based pyramid

vertex

edge

face

Did you know?

Polyhedra are made up of faces, edges and **vertices** (corners).
A cube has 6 faces, 12 edges and 8 vertices.
A Swiss mathematician called Euler discovered a pattern between the faces, vertices and edges of 3D shapes.
This is his **formula**:
number of vertices – number of edges + number of faces = 2
$(V - E) + F = 2$
Try it with other 3D shapes.

Kite Flight

It was perfect kite-flying weather, and Isabella watched as a group of children controlled their kites skilfully, making them soar, swoop and spin.

"I'm sure I can do that," she thought. "It looks easy." She asked Max if he would help her make a kite.

"Only if I can make one myself. Perhaps we can see which kite is the best flier," he replied.

They found some tissue paper, wooden rods, glue, sticky tape and string and laid it all out on the kitchen table. "I think a kite needs to be shaped like a kite," said Isabella, mysteriously.

kite

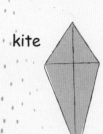

"Well, obviously…" Max replied. "An elephant shape may be tricky."

"I mean a kite – a 4-sided shape with the sides next to each other the same length." Isabella realised that Max was smiling and knew what she was talking about.

"Yes, a kite has **adjacent** sides equal, but it could be a rhombus, with all the sides equal length," said Max.

Isabella wasn't sure how a rhombus was different to a square, until Max explained that a rhombus had opposite angles equal, but no right angles. "It looks like a square when it is this way up," explained Max, holding the cut-out rhombus by one of the corners, "but if you turn it on its side it looks like a flattened parallelogram."

rhombus

rhombus   parallelogram

Isabella looked at the shapes they had cut out. "Do you realise all these shapes are **quadrilaterals**?" she exclaimed.

Max liked to think he was a little bit creative. "I've worked out my design," he announced. He folded up the bottom of the kite shape and stuck down the triangle.

"I've folded over this **isosceles triangle** for extra reinforcement, and made a perfect pentagon kite. I think you'll find this provides optimum speed and control."

Isabella wasn't convinced. "Let's go and test them…"

Perhaps I'll try a triangle next time!

Top Tips

2D shapes with straight sides are called **polygons**.
The name of the polygon tells you the number of sides it has:

Number of sides	Name
3	Triangle
4	Quadrilateral
5	Pentagon
6	Hexagon
7	Heptagon
8	Octagon

Regular polygons are shapes with all sides and angles equal.

Did you know?

The **diameter** is the distance right across a circle.
The **radius** is the distance from the centre of a circle to the edge.
The **circumference** is the distance all the way round a circle.
Remember: the diameter is double the radius.

A Pile of Tiles

The kitchen floor was being replaced with new, rectanglular tiles. The builder tried different designs, but none of them looked good on the floor.

Isabella knew that her computer had a good design program, so she decided to help the builder. She went up to the office and found the program. She drew a rectangle, copied it, clicked on one corner and rotated the new tile 90° **clockwise**. She repeated this four times until she had an interesting design.

Sir Ralph watched Isabella working on the computer. "Why don't you group these tiles and then **translate** the shape?" he asked.

Isabella looked blank. "Can you say that in English, please?"

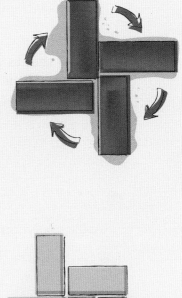

"Group and slide. Let me show you," Sir Ralph said as he took the mouse. With a few clicks and key presses he had several repeats of the shape. "A translation is just another word for a slide. The shape is slid across or down, or both, without rotating it."

Isabella took over again and made an interesting **tessellation** – pattern – with the tiles. She was sure the builder would like this design.

When they went back down to the kitchen, the builder had already started on his design. Isabella was dismayed, but realised that her design may have been a little complicated. This was a simple design but looked very good.

"Oh look," exclaimed Isabella. "It's a tile pattern made from a translation and a 90° rotation."

The builder looked at her and scratched his head. "I'll try to remember that. It sounds so much better than its usual name: herringbone pattern."

Did someone mention bones?

Top Tips

A shape can be moved by:

Translation: this is sliding a shape without rotating or flipping over.

Rotation: a shape can be rotated about a point, clockwise or **anti-clockwise**.

Reflection: this is sometimes called flipping.

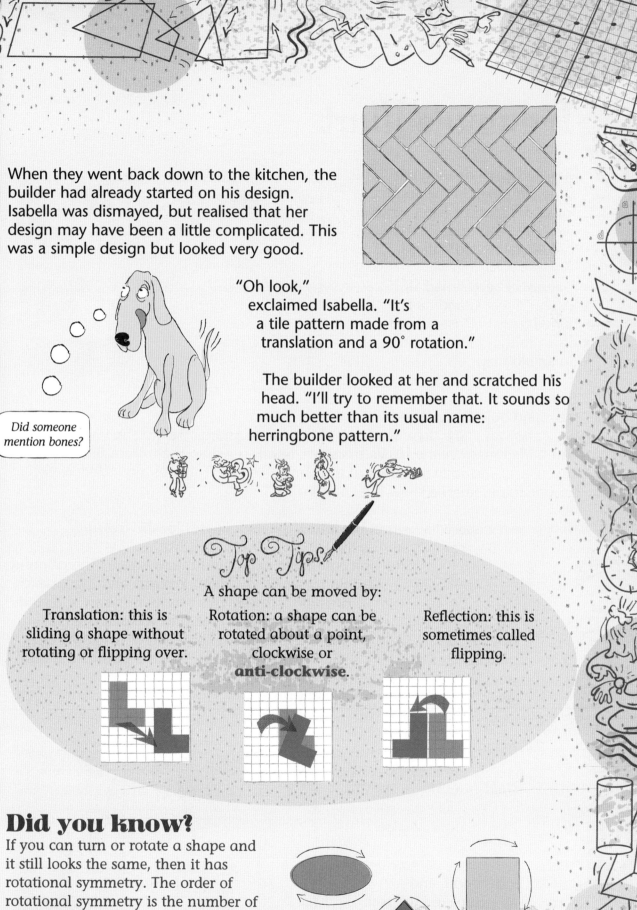

Did you know?

If you can turn or rotate a shape and it still looks the same, then it has rotational symmetry. The order of rotational symmetry is the number of times the shape can turn and still look the same.

Treasure Hunt

Max had been clearing out some old boxes in the South Tower. He found a letter written over 100 years ago. He showed it to Sir Ralph and Isabella.

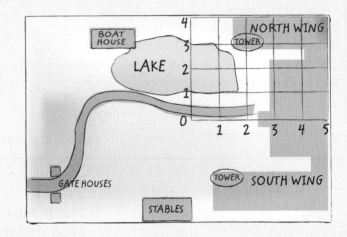

"Fantastic!" exclaimed Sir Ralph. "Great Grandma Lizzy's buried treasure!" He rushed down to the cellar and brought up an old map.

Sir Ralph saw their amazed faces and quickly explained what this was. "She drew this map of our house and garden to show where she had buried many of the family treasures. She was hiding them from her husband because he was spending a lot of the family fortune. This was a good idea, except for one thing: no-one knew the coordinates."

Max now realised what was in the letter: the coordinates for the treasure.

Sir Ralph continued explaining the mystery. "The painting was hidden at (2, 3). That's 2 across and 3 up, which is the North Tower. This was found years ago, and everywhere else on the grid was searched for more treasure. But clever Great Grandma Lizzy buried the rest of the treasure outside the grid that she had drawn!"

Painting (2, 3)

Silver (0, −4)

Diamonds (−5, −3)

Gold (−3, 3)

Max understood, and carefully completed the rest of the coordinates grid.

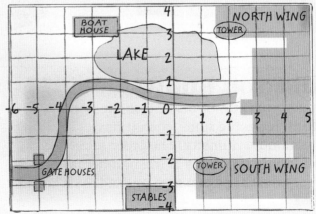

Isabella was still confused. "So where is (0, −4)?"

"The zero shows that you stay at zero, and −4 means 4 squares down – the corner of the stables," explained Max.

Now she could see how the negative numbers were used. "So the diamonds are 5 squares to the left of zero and 3 squares down, which is the gatehouse, and the gold is …"

"Exactly," interrupted Sir Ralph and Max together, before rushing out to find some spades.

They knew it was only a small amount of family treasure, but it was great to solve the 100-year-old mystery!

Brilliant! I've been looking for that for ages!

Top Tips

Coordinates are always written in brackets and separated by a comma. The numbers on the horizontal x-**axis** are written first, then the vertical y-axis. A way to remember this is that x comes before y.

Did you know?

The **vertices** of shapes can be drawn on a coordinates grid. You may be asked to complete a shape and plot the coordinates. Use a ruler to help, and look carefully at the positions of each vertex to check that they are correct.

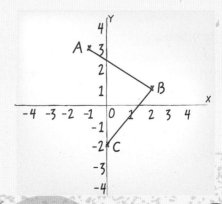

House Hunt

For her homework, Isabella was asked to go on a right angle hunt around the house. She searched the kitchen and found four on the door and more on cupboard corners.

Max was in the kitchen, cooking. "How do you know they are right angles?" he asked.

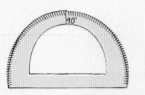

Isabella explained that she could spot right angles because they were $\frac{1}{4}$ of a complete turn in a circle, which is 90 degrees (°). She also had a protractor to measure angles, but was struggling to use this in the corners of the room.

Max tore off a piece of paper, folded it exactly in half and then in half again.

"There," he said, "a right angle checker."

Isabella found this a lot easier to use, but was surprised when she found that the corner of the room wasn't a right angle.

"These old houses have walls at all sorts of strange angles," Max explained. "This is actually an **obtuse angle**, leaning out so it is greater than 90°. If the wall was leaning in so it was less than a right angle it would be called an **acute angle**."

obtuse angle   acute angle

A cute angle? I'm the cute one round here.

Isabella continued hunting for right angles and spotted one in a triangle wall tile. "This triangle is special. It has two acute angles and a right angle," she told Max.

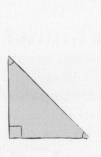

Max explained that there was something else special about the angles of a triangle. "No matter what type of triangle, the three angles always add up to 180°."

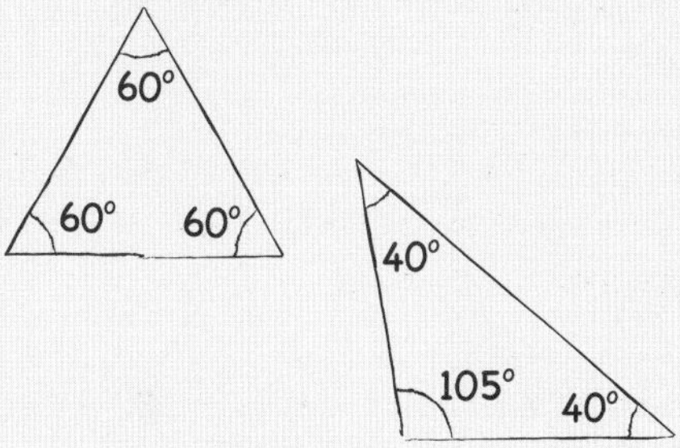

He drew two triangles for Isabella to check with her protractor.

Max then showed a way to test this. He cut out a triangle and tore each of the angles off. He then laid them next to each other and they cleverly made a straight line – 180°.

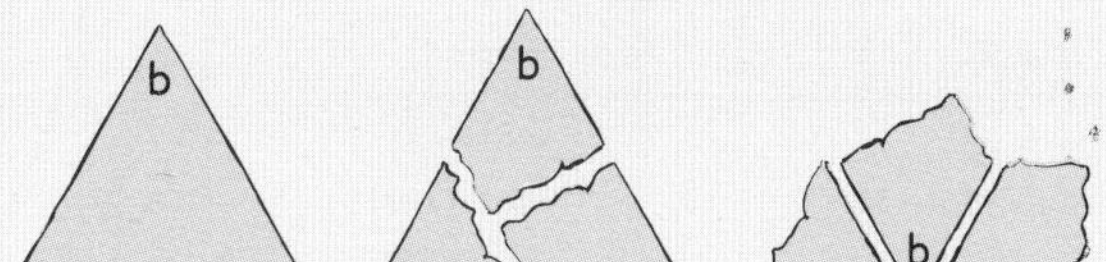

Top Tips!

These are the key angles to recognise and learn:

360° full circle   90° right angle 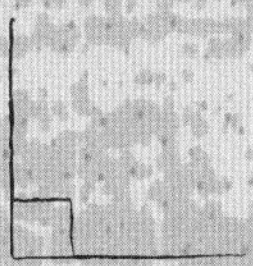   Between 90° and 180° obtuse angle

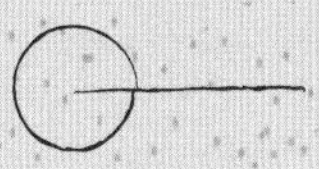

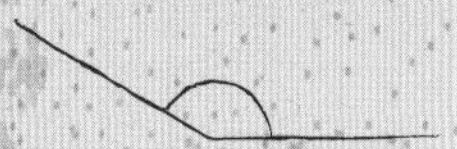

180° straight line 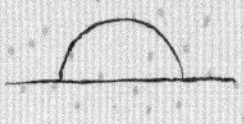   Less than 90° acute angle 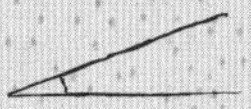   Between 180° and 360° **reflex angle**

Did you know?

When straight lines meet or cross they follow certain angle rules:

Angles on a straight line total 180°   Angles at a point total 360° 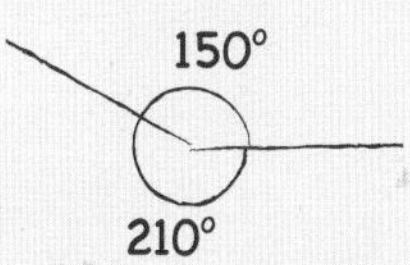   When two straight lines cross, the opposite angles are equal

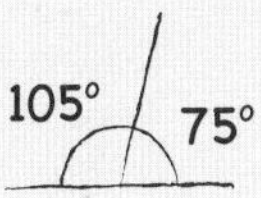

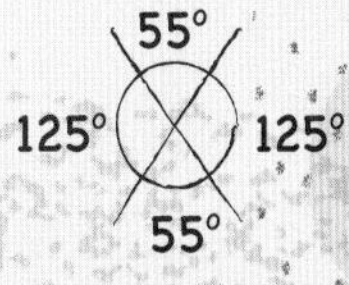

105° 75°   150° 210°   55° 125° 125° 55°

Quadrilaterals

square rectangle rhombus

kite parallelogram trapezium

Triangles

equilateral isosceles scalene right angle

Number of sides	Name	Number of sides	Name
3	triangle	7	heptagon
4	quadrilateral	8	octagon
5	pentagon	9	nonagon
6	hexagon	10	decagon

180°
(straight line)

90°
(right angle)

acute angle
(less than a
right angle)

obtuse angle
(between 90°
and 180°)

reflex angle
(between 180°
and 360°)

Angles on
straight
add up
to 180°

Angles at
point add
up to 36

Types of

Shapes

Measuring

All the angles in
a triangle add up
to 180°

$a + b + c = 180°$

All the angles in
a quadrilateral
add up to 360°

$a + b + c + d = 360°$

circles

circumference

Count the degree lines carefully. This angle is 75°

Read from
0° on the
outer scale

Place the cross at the point of
the angle you are measuring

Quadrilaterals

Triangles

Polygons

shapes with straight sides

Circles

2D shapes

using
protra

SH

translation

reflection

rotation

mirror line

movement geometry

3D shapes

Cube:
6 faces
12 edge
8 vertic

vertex

face

edge

names

parts of 3D shapes

nets

cube cuboid cylinder tetrahedron

cone triangular
prism sphere square-based
pyramid

Two different
nets of cubes

COORDINA

Read across
then up or down

4 quadrants

A → (-2, 1)

B → (3, 1)

C → (5, -2)

D → (-4, -2)

x then y

1 minute = 60 seconds
1 hour = 60 minutes
1 day = 24 hours
1 week = 7 days
1 fortnight = 14 days
1 year = 12 months = 365 days
leap year = 366 days

105° 75°

150°

6cm
4cm
Area = 24cm²

Area of rectangle
= length × width

Area = 9 squares

8cm
5cm   5cm
8cm
Distance round edge = 26cm

Direction

NW N NE
W   E
SW S SE

Compass

Area

Perimeter

a
b
Perimeter of rectangle
= 2 (a+b)

AREA + PERIMETER

SHAPE + MEASURES

Length	Mass	Capacity
12 inches = 1 foot	16 ounces = 1 pound (lb)	8 pints = 1 gallon
2.5cm ≈ 1 inch	25g ≈ 1 ounce	1.75 pints ≈ 1 litre
30cm ≈ 1 foot	2.25lb ≈ 1kg	4.5 litres ≈ 1 gallon
3 feet ≈ 1 metre		

≈ means 'is approximately equal to'

Imperial measures

Length

MEASURES

Mass

Capacity

Length

1 centimetre (cm) = 10 millimetres (mm)
1 metre (m) = 100cm
1 kilometre (km) = 1000m

Mass

1 kilogram (kg) = 1000 grams (g)
1 tonne = 1000kg

Capacity

1 litre (l) = 1000 millilitres (ml)
1 centilitre (cl) = 100ml

TIME

Telling the time

Time facts

24-hr time

o'clock
55 minutes past   5 minutes past
50 minutes past   12   10 minutes past
                11   1
45 minutes past 10   2 15 minutes past
                9   3
40 minutes past   8   4 20 minutes past
                7 6 5
35 minutes past   25 minutes past
      30 minutes past

am : ante meridian
(morning)

pm : post meridian
(afternoon/evening)

12 hour clock	midnight		am		noon		pm		midnight
	12 1 2 3 4 5 6 7 8 9 10 11			12 1 2 3 4 5 6 7 8 9 10 11			12			

24 hour clock		
	0 1 2 3 4 5 6 7 8 9 10 11 12 13 14 15 16 17 18 19 20 21 22 23 24	

9.45 am is written as 0945
9.45 pm is written as 2145

Revise Time

1 Join the equivalent measures.

a	1.8km	18mm
b	6700ml	6.75kg
c	1.8cm	1800m
d	180cm	6.71
e	6750g	1m 80cm

2 Complete this bus timetable. Each bus takes the same time as the other buses between stops.

	BUS 1	BUS 2	BUS 3
Station	08:40	12:54	17:36
Hospital	08:59	_____	_____
School	_____	13:50	_____
Park	_____	_____	19:12

3 Calculate the area and perimeter of this shape.

a Perimeter = _____

b Area = _____

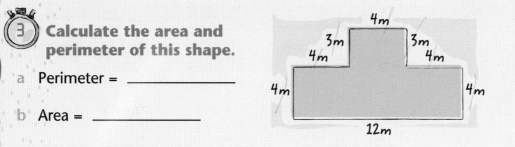

4 Tick the correct boxes to show whether these are prisms or pyramids.

Shape	A	B	C	D	E	F
Prism	☐	☐	☐	☐	☐	☐
Pyramid	☐	☐	☐	☐	☐	☐

5 Match each name to the shape.

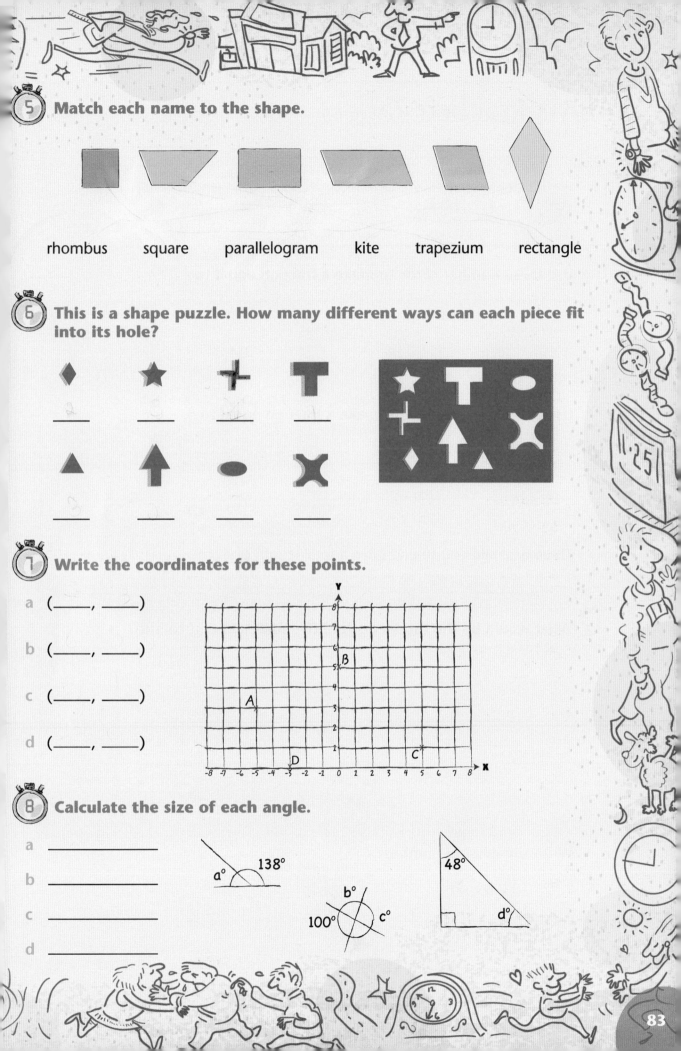

rhombus   square   parallelogram   kite   trapezium   rectangle

6 This is a shape puzzle. How many different ways can each piece fit into its hole?

_____   _____   _____   _____

_____   _____   _____   _____

7 Write the coordinates for these points.

a (_____, _____)

b (_____, _____)

c (_____, _____)

d (_____, _____)

8 Calculate the size of each angle.

a _____

b _____

c _____

d _____

138°

a°

100°   b°   c°

48°

d°

SATs Practice Paper

| 4 | 3 | 8 | 12 | 10 | 6 |

1 Use these number cards to make a fraction equal to $\frac{1}{3}$.

$$\frac{\square}{\square}$$

2 Use two different cards to make a fraction equal to $\frac{3}{4}$.

$$\frac{\square}{\square}$$

3 Three nails laid end-to-end have a total length of 42cm.

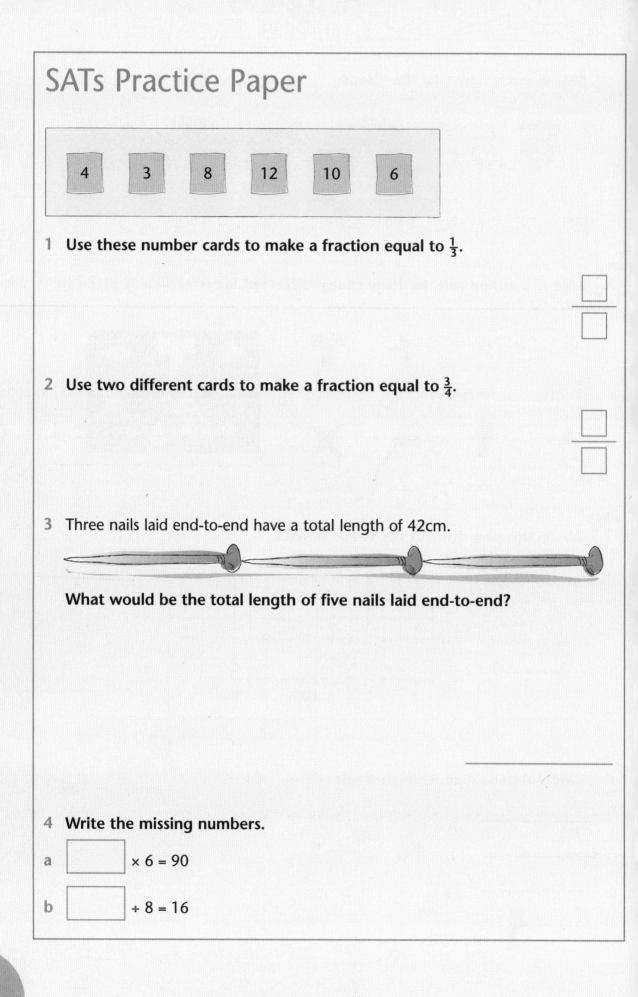

What would be the total length of five nails laid end-to-end?

_____

4 Write the missing numbers.

a $\boxed{} \times 6 = 90$

b $\boxed{} \div 8 = 16$

In a school fête these are the amounts collected at five children's stalls.

£5.15   £4.35   £4.25   £5.10   £8.65

5   **What is the mean average amount collected from these five stalls?**

Show your method. You may get a mark.

_____

6   These five stalls raised 10% of the total amount of money raised by the fête.

How much money did the fête raise altogether?

_____

7   The fête opened at 1.45pm and finished at 4.30pm.

How many minutes in total was the fête open for?

_____

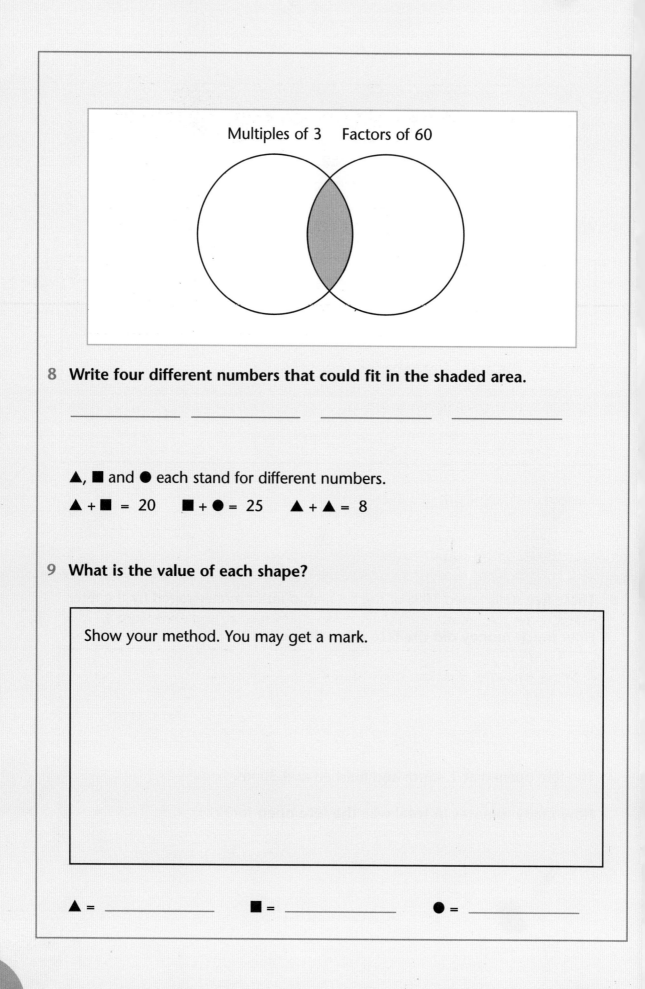

Multiples of 3   Factors of 60

8 **Write four different numbers that could fit in the shaded area.**

_____ _____ _____ _____

▲, ■ and ● each stand for different numbers.

▲ + ■ = 20   ■ + ● = 25   ▲ + ▲ = 8

9 **What is the value of each shape?**

Show your method. You may get a mark.

▲ = _____   ■ = _____   ● = _____

This is a tile design of a small square inside a larger square.

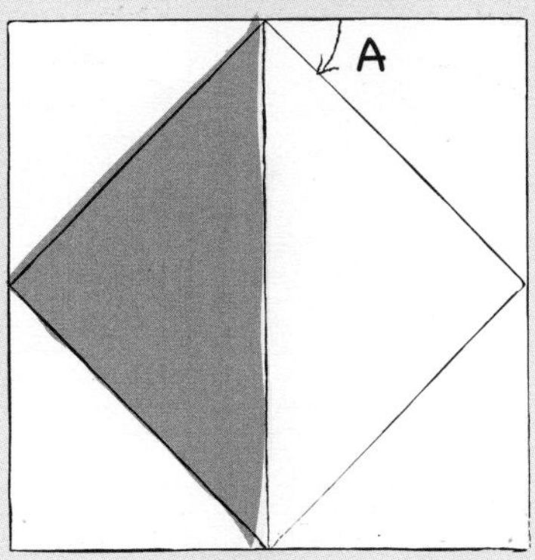

10 Calculate the area of the shaded part of the tile.

a Perimeter of smaller square = 56cm

b Area of shaded part = _____ cm²

Explain how you worked it out.

_____

_____

11 What is the size of angle A? Do not use a protractor (angle measurer).

Show your method. You may get a mark.

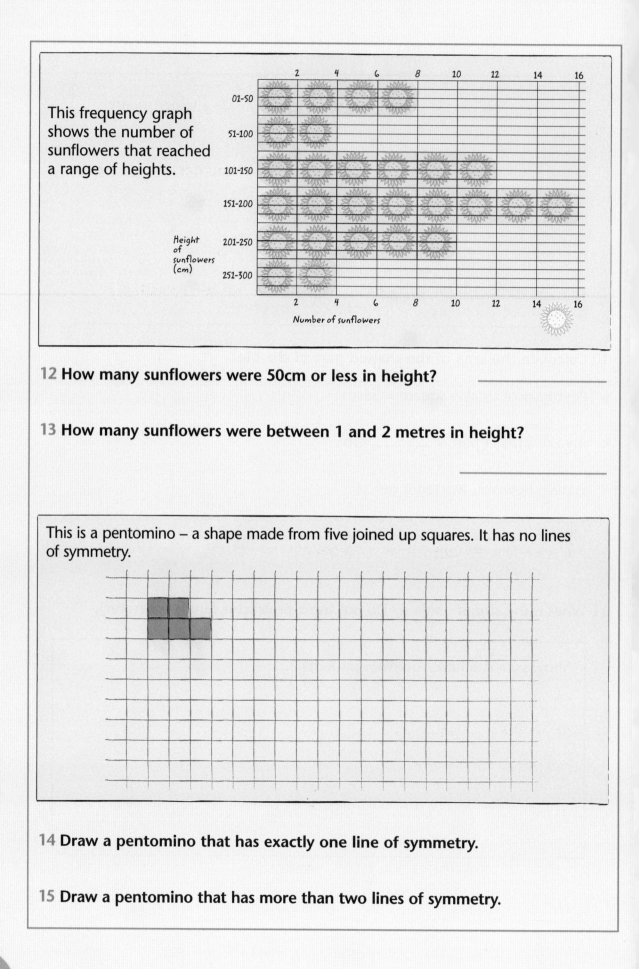

This frequency graph shows the number of sunflowers that reached a range of heights.

Height of sunflowers (cm)

01-50 · 51-100 · 101-150 · 151-200 · 201-250 · 251-300

Number of sunflowers

12 How many sunflowers were 50cm or less in height? _____

13 How many sunflowers were between 1 and 2 metres in height?

_____

This is a pentomino – a shape made from five joined up squares. It has no lines of symmetry.

14 Draw a pentomino that has exactly one line of symmetry.

15 Draw a pentomino that has more than two lines of symmetry.

There are 12 coloured counters in a bag: 5 blue, 4 red, 2 green and 1 yellow.

16 Circle the fraction that shows the proportion of counters that are green.

$$\frac{1}{5} \qquad \frac{1}{2} \qquad \frac{1}{6} \qquad \frac{2}{5}$$

17 Tick the arrow on the probability scale that shows the probability of randomly picking out a red counter.

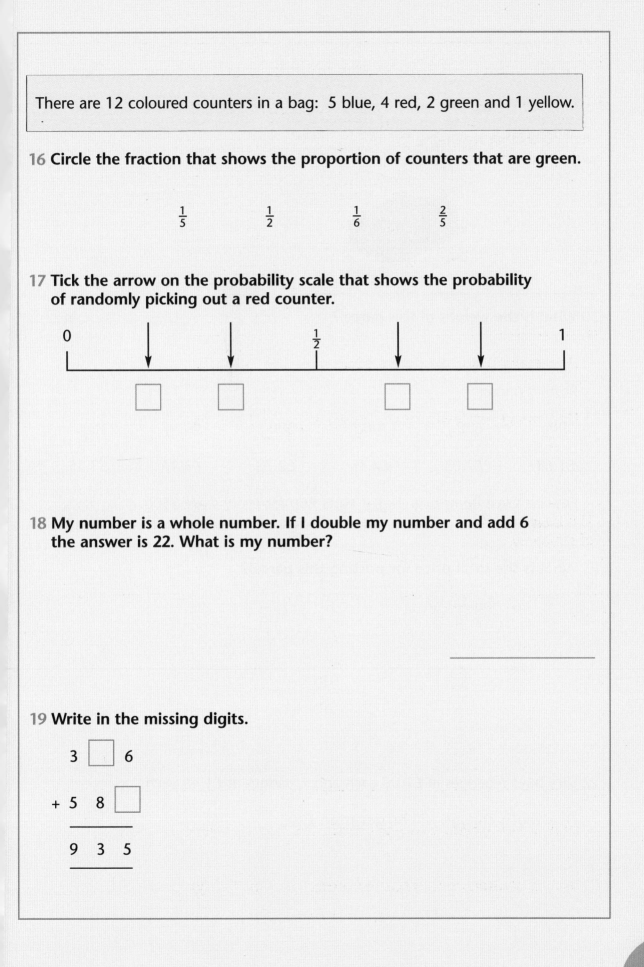

18 My number is a whole number. If I double my number and add 6 the answer is 22. What is my number?

_____

19 Write in the missing digits.

```
   3 ☐ 6
+  5 8 ☐
  ───────
   9 3 5
```

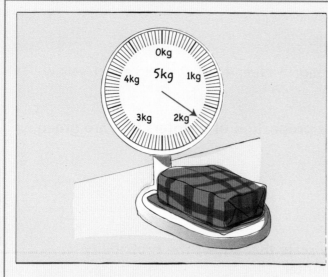

20 What is the weight of this parcel? _____

Posting prices:

500g	600g	700g	800g	900g	1kg
£1.68	£2.03	£2.38	£2.73	£3.10	£3.45

For First Class items over 1kg, it costs 86p for every extra 250g.

21 What is the total price for posting this parcel?

_____

22 Sam buys 6 badges at £1.09 each and 7 badges at £1.45 each.

How much change will he get from £20?

_____

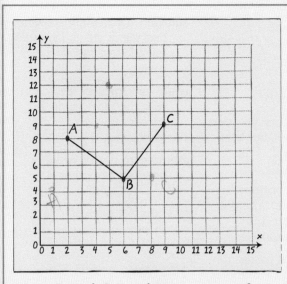

23 A, B and C are three corners of a square.

What are the coordinates of the other corner, D?

_____ , _____

24 Another square is plotted as a translation of square A, B, C, D.

If A is now at (1, 4) and C is at (8, 5), what are the coordinates of position B?

_____ , _____

The formula for a number pattern is: b = 2a − 1

25 **Write in the missing numbers.**

a   1   2   3   4   5

b   1   _____   _____   _____   9

Glossary

abacus a simple calculating tool. Beads or rings are used to count and calculate

acute angle an angle less than 90°

adjacent near or next to something

anti-clockwise turning in this direction, opposite to the hands of a clock

approximate an approximate answer is very close to the right answer, but not exact. The sign for 'approximately equal to' is ≈

area the area of a shape is the amount of surface that it covers

axis the horizontal or vertical line on a graph

circumference the distance all the way round a circle

clockwise turning in this direction, like the hands of a clock

consecutive numbers numbers that follow one after the other, in order

denominator the bottom number of a fraction; the number of parts it is divided into. Example: $\frac{2}{3}$

diameter a line that passes from one side of a circle to the other through the centre

difference the amount by which one number is greater than another

digit there are 10 digits: 0 1 2 3 4 5 6 7 8 and 9 that make all the numbers we use

discount the amount subtracted from the original price of an item

divisible if one number can be divided exactly by another number then it is divisible by this number

dodecahedron a solid shape with 12 faces. The faces of a regular dodecahedron are regular pentagons

edge where two faces of a 3D shape meet

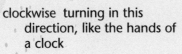

edge

equation a statement showing that things are equal, usually using letters and always having an equals sign

equivalent fraction a fraction with the same value as another fraction. Example: $\frac{3}{12} = \frac{1}{4}$

estimate to decide roughly how big a number is

face the flat sides of a 3D shape

face

factor a number that will divide exactly into other numbers. Example: 5 is a factor of 20

formula a formula (plural – formulae) uses letters or words to give a rule

function a rule for changing one set of numbers into another. For example, the function ×5 changes 3 to 15 and 20 to 100. Function machines can be drawn to show numbers coming in and out with a function in the machine.

inverse operations the inverse is the opposite and the four operations are +, −, ×, and ÷. The inverse of addition is subtraction and the inverse of multiplication is division

isosceles triangle a triangle with two equal sides and equal opposite base angles

likelihood the likelihood of something happening is the chance or probability of it happening

mean average the total divided by the number of items. Example: the mean of 3, 1, 6 and 2 is $(3 + 1 + 6 + 2) \div 4 = 3$

median the middle number in an ordered list. Example: 5, 9, 16, 18, 19. The median number is 16

mode the most common number in a list. Example: 2, 5, 4, 2, 3, 5, 2. The mode is 2

multiple a number made by multiplying together two other numbers

net the net of a 3D shape is what it looks like when it is opened out flat

numerator the top number of a fraction; the number of parts that are taken Example: $\frac{3}{5}$

obtuse angle an angle between 90° and 180°

perimeter the distance all the way round the edge of a shape or object

pi (π) if the circumference of a circle is divided by its diameter the answer is always equal to pi. It is approximately equal to 3.142

π = circumference ÷ diameter

place value the place or position of a digit in a number. The same digit has a different value at different places in the number

polygon any 2D shape with straight sides

polyhedron a many-sided solid shape with flat sides

prime number a number that can only be divided exactly by either itself or 1

proportion the proportion of an amount is the same as finding a fraction of the whole amount. For example, in a box of chocolates, 4 out of 12 chocolates are caramel. The proportion of caramel chocolates is $\frac{4}{12}$ or $\frac{1}{3}$

quadrilateral any flat shape with 4 straight sides

radius the distance from the centre of a circle to the edge

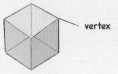

range the difference between the greatest and least values, showing the spread of data

ratio ratio compares one part or amount with another. For example, in a kitchen, if for every 2 white tiles there were 3 blue tiles, the ratio of white to blue is 2:3

reflex angle an angle greater than 180°

rounding rounding a number means changing it to the nearest ten, hundred or thousand, or changing a decimal to the nearest tenth, hundredth or thousandth to give an approximate number

sequence a row of numbers. The next number in a sequence is found by applying a rule to the previous number

square number a number multiplied by itself makes a square number Example: $4 \times 4 = 4^2 = 16$

tessellation a pattern made by fitting together flat shapes or tiles so that there are no gaps

translation a movement of a shape in a straight line, up down or at an angle. Every point of a shape that is translated moves the same distance and direction.

triangular number a number made by triangle patterns. Example: $1 + 2 = 3$, $1 + 2 + 3 = 6$

vertex the corner of a 3D shape, where edges meet (plural – vertices)

vertex

Answers

Pages 22–23 Revision exercises

Exercise 1
The code is: top banana

Exercise 2

×	6	8	9	3
9	54	72	81	27
7	42	56	63	21
4	24	32	36	12
5	30	40	45	15

Exercise 3
a 17.24 119.3   c 45.84
b 225.78

Exercise 4
a 1.38m   c 0.98m
b 2.36m

Exercise 5

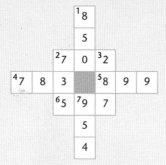

Exercise 6
a
$$3 \overline{\smash{)}126} = 42$$

b
$$5 \overline{\smash{)}865} = 173$$

c
$$4 \overline{\smash{)}768} = 192$$

Exercise 7
Check answers – various answers are possible.

Exercise 8
a 9 – (4 + 3) = 2
b (24 ÷ 3) × 4 = 32
c (7 × 4) – (3 + 6) = 19
d (18 – 2) × (4 + 2) = 96

Pages 42–43 Revision exercises

Exercise 1
a 74050   c 1430
b 3070   d 29.61

Exercise 2
a –13, –8, –6, –5, –1, 0, 2
b 15°C
c 7°C

Exercise 3
a $\frac{4}{5} = \frac{20}{25}, \frac{3}{4} = \frac{15}{20}, \frac{3}{10} = \frac{30}{100}, \frac{1}{3} = \frac{3}{9}, \frac{3}{8} = \frac{6}{16}$
b $\frac{4}{5}, \frac{20}{25}, \frac{3}{4}, \frac{15}{20}$

Exercise 4
a $\frac{2}{5} > \frac{1}{4} = \frac{4}{16} < \frac{3}{10} < \frac{1}{2}$
b 0.2 > 0.15 > 0.08 < 0.81 < 0.9
c $\frac{1}{5} = 0.2 < \frac{7}{10} > 0.07 < \frac{3}{5}$

Exercise 5

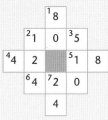

Exercise 6

a 6 petals: $\frac{1}{5}$, 4 petals: $\frac{1}{2}$, 12 petals: $\frac{3}{10}$

b blue : red 1 : 6
white : red 1 : 2
blue : white 1 : 3

Exercise 7

0.08   0.54   0.9

Exercise 8

fraction	percentage	decimal
$\frac{2}{5}$	40%	0.4
$\frac{1}{4}$	25%	0.25
$\frac{4}{5}$	80%	0.8

Pages 62–63 Revision exercises

Exercise 1

a 23, 18, 13, 8, 3, –2, –7, –12
b 8, 17, 26, 35, 44, 53, 62, 71
c 1, 4, 9, 16, 25, 36, 49, 64

Exercise 2

124   372   ⑵⑴⑸   608
441   816   243   392

Exercise 3

a n = 5   **c** a = 27
b y = 11   **d** x = 3

Exercise 4

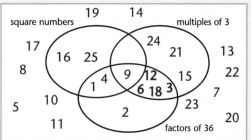

Exercise 5

a $\frac{1}{3}$ or 1 in 3   **c** $\frac{1}{2}$ or 1 in 2
b $\frac{1}{4}$ or 1 in 4

Exercise 6

a June   **d** March
b August   **e** April
c May   **f** September

Exercise 7

June

Exercise 8

a 17°C   **c** 17°C
b 16°C

Pages 82–83 Revision exercises

Exercise 1

a 1.8km – 1800m
b 6700ml – 6.7l
c 1.8cm – 18mm
d 180cm – 1m 80cm
e 6750g – 6.75kg

Exercise 2

a

Bus 1	Bus 2	Bus 3
08:40	12:54	17:36
08:59	13:13	17:55
09:36	13:50	18:32
10:16	14:30	19:12

Exercise 3

a Perimeter = 38m   **b** Area = 60m^2

Exercise 4
a prism
b pyramid
c pyramid
d prism
e pyramid
f prism

Exercise 5

rhombus   square

parallelogram   kite

trapezium   rectangle

Exercise 6

◆ = 2   ★ = 5

✚ = 4   T = 1

▲ = 3   ⬆ = 1

⬭ = 2   ✕ = 4

Exercise 7
a (–5, 3)   b (0, 5)   c (5, 1)   d (–3, 0)

Exercise 8
a 42°   c 100°
b 80°   d 42°

Pages 84–91 SATs practice paper

1 $\frac{4}{12}$

2 $\frac{6}{8}$

3 70cm

4 a $15 \times 6 = 90$
   b $128 \div 8 = 16$

5 £5.50

6 £275

7 165 minutes

8 Any four from 3, 6, 12, 15, 30, 60

9 ▲ = 4, ■ = 16, ● = 9

10 98 cm^2

11 45°

12 8

13 28

14 Check answers

15 Check answers

16 $\frac{1}{6}$

17

18 8

19
```
    3 4 6
  + 5 8 9
  -------
    9 3 5
```

20 1750g

21 £6.03

22 £3.31

23 (5, 12)

24 (5, 1)

25 1, 3, 5, 7, 9